Historic Tales

— of —

ST. LOUIS

MARK ZEMAN

THE
History
PRESS

Published by The History Press
Charleston, SC
www.historypress.com

Copyright © 2023 by Mark Zeman
All rights reserved

Front cover: Missouri Historical Society.
Back cover, top: Missouri Historical Society; *bottom*: Missouri Historical Society.

Unless otherwise noted, all images are courtesy of the author.

First published 2023

Manufactured in the United States

ISBN 9781467153287

Library of Congress Control Number: 2022944986

CONTENTS

CONTENTS

CONTENTS

Contents

PREFACE

S t. Louis owes its existence to its geographic location, the convergence of two great rivers at the doorway to a bounty of natural resources. Its growth was driven by easterners who rolled the dice on huge risks, lured by equally huge potentials for gain. Ideally situated between supply and demand, this location proved to be the ideal conduit for movement and trade, much like the Panama Canal or the Silk Road, where fortunes were made at the crossroads of capital investment, hard work and being in the right place at the right time.

Among the city's many treasures is the collection of mosaics at the Cathedral Basilica—forty-one million tiny slivers of colored glass, no two alike, featuring seven thousand colors and covering eighty-three thousand square feet. The building houses the largest collection of mosaics outside of Russia. Viewing a mosaic from afar, you see the splendor of the forms and colors; walking closer, you begin to see the detail and individual fragments. And, getting even closer, you see individual chips and irregularities and cubes of color with no seeming relationship of one to the next. Nothing fits, and it forms an indiscernible hodgepodge. All those bits, some too close together, some fractured and chipped—only when we step back do our eyes blend them together so we can view them collectively as a cohesive image.

Such is history. There is no such thing as definitive history; there is only examining certain events while being unable to see (or choosing to ignore) others. This book lays out little pieces of St. Louis that for the most part are not discussed elsewhere; the vignettes instead mostly focus on obscure and often forgotten details of our past. Many chapters are an intricate interweaving of seemingly unrelated events, painting a picture vastly different from textbook histories, whose tidy summaries, abundant with omission, fuel our misconceptions. Other chapters are brief snippets of intriguing history that add further flavor to our understanding.

By examining the minutiae and backstory of St. Louis' history, this work enables the reader to see our collective accomplishments, the circumstances and the oddities—often coupled with the less admirable qualities of our predecessors. The study of such events creates the opportunity for introspection and to gain a new perspective into our beliefs and values.

You may find some of the stories intriguing, fascinating or humorous. One thing is certain: after reading this book, you will not be unchanged.

Detail of a mosaic from St. Louis' Cathedral Basilica.

ARMY SECRETLY SPRAYS ST. LOUIS IN CHEMICAL WEAPONS PROGRAM

*I*n 1953 and 1963–65, the U.S. Army Chemical Corps secretly sprayed American cities with zinc cadmium sulfide particles to test chemical warfare technology. In total, it conducted 160 tests at sixty-six locations in the United States using various substances. The program, named Operation Large Area Coverage (LAC), was to monitor the dispersal patterns of airborne particles for their effectiveness.

Test sites across the country were selected based on their similarity to cities in the Soviet Union. One city was St. Louis. Here the army employed three dispersion methods: motorized blowers on top of buildings, station wagons and aircraft. The building tests were conducted from tall buildings, including the Pruitt-Igoe public housing facility, home to ten thousand low-income residents, most Black, of which 70 percent were under the age of twelve.

The operation was covert, and the army informed local officials that the chemical dispersal was simply to test a smoke screen that would shield St. Louis from aerial reconnaissance during a possible Soviet attack.

The true nature of the chemical test was exposed in 1994. In many areas in the United States and Canada, a fine powder of fluorescent zinc cadmium sulfide and other chemicals had been sprayed as part of an offensive biological weapons program.

In 1996, Congress ordered the National Research Council to conduct a health study in areas that were exposed. The council determined that the tests did not expose residents to harmful levels of the chemical. However, it

A C-119 Flying Boxcar, the type of plane used to release fluorescent zinc cadmium sulfide. *U.S. Air Force.*

conceded that the research was limited and the findings were based on data from animal testing.

The council did acknowledge that high doses of cadmium over long periods could cause bone and kidney problems and lung cancer. It recommended follow-up studies to obtain a more accurate assessment of the effect of the spray on humans.

AUTOMOBILES AND ROADS

*T*here is an old saying applied to St. Louis (but not *by* St. Louisans): "First in shoes, first in booze and last in the American League." Ouch. Baseball aside, this line references the city's uncontested leadership in the shoe manufacturing and brewery businesses. Lesser known but equally valid is St. Louis' role in the production of coffee, bricks, fur and automobiles.

In the mid-1920s, St. Louis had a whopping twenty-seven auto manufacturing companies as well as numerous suppliers, amounting to roughly 20 percent of the city's economy. While Detroit had the big mass production companies—General Motors, Ford and Chrysler—St. Louis firms specialized in high quality vehicles, with producers like the Gardner Motor Company, the Moon Motor Car Company and the Saint Louis Motor Carriage Company (Dorris) on Locust Street. They produced significantly fewer cars but with higher quality. Dorris's motto was, "Built up to a standard, not down to a price." The cars were exceptional, but they cost as much as ten times the price of a new Ford Model T. When the Great Depression hit, they weren't long for this world.

In the 1950s, St. Louis was again a major manufacturing center, second only to Detroit, with major plants in Fenton (Chrysler), Hazelwood (Ford) and Wentzville (General Motors, which manufactured the Corvette).

Along with the vehicle itself, St. Louis had to build the infrastructure to support the automobile: roads, bridges, repair shops and gas stations. Fueling a car was a serious issue in the early days. You had to bring a bucket or tin

Left: A 1917 Dorris 1-B-6 Opera Coupe. It was designed with enough headroom for gentlemen to wear a top hat while going to the opera. Photo taken at the National Museum of Transportation, 2020.

Right: The first filling station in the world, 1905. *Missouri Historical Society*.

can to a pharmacy, hardware store or refinery to be filled. Some clever fellow came up with the idea of toting barrels of gasoline on roadways to fill tanks with a hose. (This doesn't seem particularly safe.)

In 1905, two enterprising men from St. Louis, C.H. Laessig and his partner, Harry Grenner, conceived of a considerably more convenient method: they put a hose on a tank at their building at 420 South Theresa Avenue. In so doing, they created the world's first purpose-built gas station. They grew their business to forty stations across St. Louis. The original building is gone, but you can still find the location.

Other entrepreneurs soon followed this model of the curbside filling station; drivers would stop right on the road and refuel. In 1900, there were only 4,000 cars in the country; by 1915, the number of vehicles had exploded to 2.3 million. With so many vehicles, stopping in the street to refuel had become a considerable problem.

The breakthrough was the drive-in gas station, where drivers could pull off the street to avoid obstructing traffic. By 1929, there were 121,513 filling stations across the country. Up to this time, the attendant fueled the car; there was no such thing as self-serve. Stations soon vied for business by offering courtesy services such as washing windows and checking oil.

Another enormous issue was the paved road. The earliest roads in St. Louis were bare dirt, and as a town grew, dirt roads were paved with brick. Thoroughfares between towns followed common horse paths, which over time were widened for wagons. Such a road was between St. Louis and St. Charles, the Rue de Roi or the King's Highway. In St. Louis, it became known as St. Charles Road, the first road to traverse the county. During heavy rains, the road became extremely muddy, so a contractor was engaged to build a plank road over it comprising horizontal timbers. Planked roads were fairly common. The 1851 Western Plank Road, stretching nine miles from Boone's Lick Trading Post to Cottleville, had a toll of "two bits" per person. The road lasted only thirteen years due to rotting timbers and thieves who stole the planks for buildings.

The next iteration was the paved road, and by 1890, St. Louis had more paved roads than almost any other city. There was an incredible lack of planning in early roads, and as the number and speed of vehicles increased, it became necessary to create arterial roadways by demolishing buildings. All the while, cities and towns slowly grew together with roads, leading to the building of early highways and freeways.

The first major effort to develop a national east–west road system was the creation of Route 66. This is a stretch of 2,500 miles of paved road that ran from downtown Chicago to Santa Monica, California. It crossed eight states and three time zones. It was often a gangly collection of roads of varying quality; in 1926, only 800 miles of Route 66 were paved. The route was not completely paved until 1937. The distinguishing characteristic of Route 66 was that it passed through seemingly every small town along the way. This gave rise to hundreds of mom-and-pop hotels in the middle of nowhere and small amusement parks. There was also the "roadside attraction," whether a giant dinosaur or the world's largest ball of twine—any curiosity that would get drivers to stop to fill up, get a meal or buy souvenirs.

Places like Ted Drewes Frozen Custard found fame and fortune on Route 66. From 1926 to 1932, the route ran through Maplewood. The city has created the "Route 66 Tribute Walk" with sidewalk plaques honoring original Route 66 businesses (7200–7400 blocks of Manchester Road). There is also a Route 66 Visitor Center (more like a museum) in Eureka, west of St. Louis.

Route 66 traveled across the Chain of Rocks Bridge; a stretch of land on the west bank of the Mississippi River there was one of several proposed as a location for the 1904 St. Louis World's Fair. In 1923, an amusement park was built here by the Parkview Amusement Company, and in 1927, it became the Chain of Rocks Amusement Park, operating until 1978. Incidentally, just south of here is the location of Camp Gaillard, the World War I camp for engineers.

The beauty of Route 66 was that you got to see lots of small-town U.S.A.—which was also its downfall. People simply wanted to get to their destination. This is one factor leading to the highways and the interstate system that we know today. These multilane, smooth and fairly straight

The Missouri side of the Chain of Rocks Bridge and Route 66, 1929. *Missouri Historical Society.*

roads intentionally bypassed small towns, driving a stake into the heart of many local businesses.

A major evolution took place with the construction of highways within the city, designed to allow traffic from the city and suburbs to bypass surface streets. The most important of these in St. Louis was Highway 40, which was run off the Poplar Street Bridge, the primary downtown bridge that connected Missouri to Illinois and the rest of the country. Strangely, in 1937, the first sections of Highway 40 originated south of Forest Park (Skinker Boulevard to Hampton, and a year later a second stretch from Kingshighway to Vandeventer). In 1938, another fourteen miles of highway between Lindbergh and the Missouri River opened, which came to be known as the Daniel Boone Expressway.

The Interstate Highway System was the natural next step in the progression of roadway evolution that had been progressing organically over many years. The nation's first section of the interstate was laid right here on August 13, 1956, in St. Charles County (then part of US Highway 40, now Interstate 70).

FIRST GAS STATION, 420 SOUTH THERESA AVENUE, ST. LOUIS, MISSOURI 63103

ST. LOUIS MOTOR CARRIAGE COMPANY, 1211–13 NORTH VANDEVENTER AVENUE, ST. LOUIS, MISSOURI 63113

ROUTE 66 VISITOR CENTER, 97 NORTH OUTER ROAD E NO. 1, EUREKA, MISSOURI 63025

THE BATTLE OF CAMP JACKSON

Suppressing a Confederate Seizure of the Union Arsenal

*H*ow did the campus of a major university get to be named after a Confederate general? It is an intriguing tale with a fascinating twist at the end.

At the onset of the American Civil War, St. Louis was the site of one of the earliest skirmishes, the Battle of Camp Jackson. The battle thwarted the Confederate Missouri militia's plans to take over the Union Arsenal. Officially, Missouri was a Union state, but its governor, Claiborne Jackson, was a secessionist. When war was declared, the governor not only refused to send volunteers to join the Union but also directed the state militia to join the Confederate army.

To this end, the militia gathered southeast of what is currently Lindell and North Grand (recently renamed Father Biondi SJ Way) to form the Confederate Camp Jackson, across the street from what is now St. Francis Xavier College Church on the campus of Saint Louis University.

To assess their strategy, on May 9, 1861, Union colonel Nathaniel Lyon, commander of the Union Arsenal, dressed as an old woman to spy on the militia. Concluding that the militia was planning to take over the armory, Colonel Lyon led Union volunteers to surround the camp and forced their surrender.

After the war, in 1874, the Lyon Monument Association donated a statue depicting Lyon on horseback accepting the surrender and placed it at West Pine and Grand (across the street from present-day DuBourg Hall).

A photo of militia units drilling at Camp Jackson, May 1861. Missouri Historical Society.

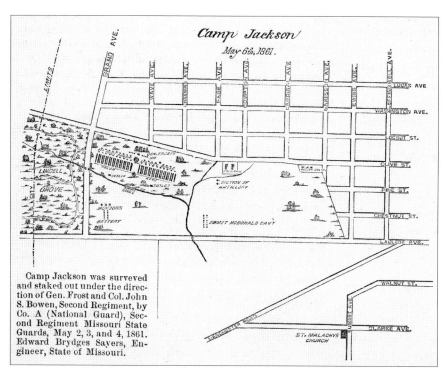

A map of Camp Jackson, placing the camp north of Lindell and east of Grand. *Missouri Historical Society.*

Here's where it starts to get interesting. Recall the Confederate general who surrendered Camp Jackson? His name was D.M. Frost. In 1959, his daughter Harriet Frost Fordyce donated $1 million to Saint Louis University (SLU), stipulating it be used to purchase twenty-two acres of land east of Grand—the same twenty-two acres occupied by Camp Jackson.

She also stipulated that it be named Frost Campus. In brief, she bought her father's Confederate camp and turned it into a SLU campus named after the Confederate general. (It has since been renamed North Campus.)

Of course, Frost's daughter had no intention of having a statue of the damn Yankee who defeated her father on his namesake campus, so in 1960, the statue was removed and relocated to Lyon Park (Broadway and Arsenal, across the street from the Anheuser-Busch brewery), on the grounds of the original arsenal (that the militia planned to capture).

The park was established in 1869. It has another monument to Lyon, an obelisk of Missouri marble that was dedicated on September 13, 1874.

THE BIRTH OF THE SUBURB

Village to Metropolis

F rom a few cabins to a village, then a town, then a city, St. Louis has experienced continuous growth and expansion. The first major expansion came in 1836, when the city sold large (forty-acre) tracts of land south and southwest of town. It held other City Subdivision land auctions in 1843, 1854 and 1855. Between 1830 and 1880, St. Louis' population grew from 8,000 to 350,000.

This exponential growth posed problems for the city, not just in demands on the infrastructure such as roads, water and sewage, but also on the pure logistics of moving people and goods. Cities up to the time of the Civil War were limited by people's ability to efficiently get to and from work and to food supplies. This was an era without refrigeration, so a housewife had to buy fresh food daily. This was also the era of shops selling just one type of product: butcher, dairy, green grocer, bakery and pharmacy. As such, a housewife had to walk to multiple locations, lugging several bags in the city's famous one-hundred-degree heat or pouring rain while wearing the cumbersome dresses of the day. Realistically, you had to live no farther than twenty to thirty minutes from work or grocers.

This all changed with the streetcar. In the 1840s, the average resident of St. Louis got around by walking (most people didn't have horses or wagons). But by the late 1850s, there was a system of horse- and mule-drawn "horsecars" on rails. In 1886, the first cable cars (cars that latched on to underground cables) were introduced, and in 1889, the first electric streetcars appeared. This latest version made it affordable for median-

The evolution in transportation: a horse-drawn wagon, streetcar and automobile on Jefferson Avenue, 1900. *Missouri History Society.*

income people to commute and conduct their daily affairs quickly and efficiently. What was once an arduous thirty-minute one-way walk became a comfortable ten-minute ride.

Where a streetcar line was run to an adjacent town, businesses sprang up to serve new customers. While a train would run nonstop between Town A and Town B, streetcars would stop frequently along the line, allowing passengers to disembark and creating business opportunities along the entire line. The businesses were in turn followed by new houses, which in turn necessitated new schools, more stores, transportation, medical facilities and other amenities and services once provided by the city. This was the creation of the "streetcar suburb," a large-scale movement of middle-income people from the inner city into newly created suburbs, which in turn resulted in the evolution of downtown into an industrial/business center. Those who remained were people without the means to pay the fares, leaving the inner city primarily to immigrants and a largely unskilled, poorer workforce. The birth of the suburb had redefined the downtown.

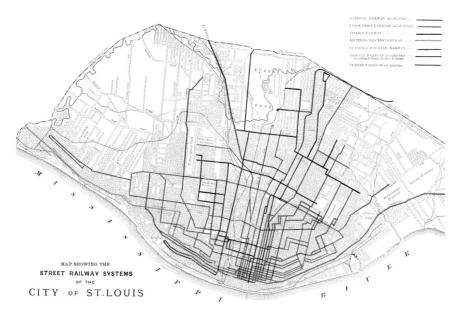

Map of the St. Louis streetcar system, 1884.

Once this phenomenon started it could not be stopped; lines were built to keep up with growing populations, creating new neighborhoods and new towns and connecting the suburbs to towns that were once far from the city center. The boom in business created opportunities for work, causing more people to move to the area.

One such suburb centered on Cherokee and Jefferson Avenues, the meeting of four neighborhoods: Benton Park, Benton Park West, Gravois Park and Marine Villa. It was the convergence of two lines of the Union Depot railroad, the electric streetcar line and Cherokee and California Avenues. A few merchants popped up, and it continued growing until it became a sizable business district that was only a seven-minute ride from downtown.

The year 1918 introduced St. Louis' first nickelodeon here, which ran silent films such as *The Romance of Tarzan and Salomé*. The next year saw the opening of the "five and ten" variety store F.W. Woolworth. Most of the area's homes were built in the 1920s and '30s.

Fred Wehrenberg is said to have opened his first theater in a bake shop here. He opened an earlier theater (1910) down the street at Cherokee and Jefferson called The Best, which had only 224 seats. Next to The Best was St. Louis' first air dome, called The Tent. The earliest films were silent movies, followed by movies with recorded music or sound effects. The first feature film that was a "talkie" was *The Jazz Singer*, which wasn't released until 1927.

That year, another famous local fixture was born, debuting as the Cinderella Recreation Hall and Dance Academy, subsequently named the Showboat Ballroom. It was sold in 1935 and renamed the Casa Loma Ballroom. Sadly, it experienced a fire in 1940, but it reopened in 1941 with a giant five-thousand-square-foot "floating" dance floor consisting of a maple dancefloor on top of an inch of rubber. The Casa Loma was one of the hottest venues in the city, showcasing the likes of Frank Sinatra, Louis Armstrong, Glenn Miller and Guy Lombardo.

BLOODY ISLAND

Submarine Telegraph Cables and a Presidential Duel

O n March 21, 1850, the last segment of telegraph cable was built between Cape Girardeau and St. Louis, the final leg of the connection between New Orleans and St. Louis. But there still wasn't a line across the Mississippi River.

The obvious next step was to connect St. Louis to the massive telegraph network east of the Mississippi. The original effort was to use "masts" to suspend telegraph wires across the river, but this proved unsuccessful. Shortly after their installation, a storm in 1848 destroyed one of the masts.

To achieve a system more resistant to the elements, the Northern and Eastern O'Reilly Telegraph Companies decided to lay cable *under* the river. On September 23, 1850, the companies laid wires encased in gutta-percha on the river's floor. (Gutta-percha is a coating of processed natural rubber made by an English company, the Gutta Percha Company, formed in 1845. The company later created the world's first international undersea telegraph cable, laid between Calais, France, and Dover, England, in 1851.)

O'Reilly chose to run the cable to St. Louis across an island that no longer exists, Bloody Island. With the river shifting over the years, the island eventually was joined to the State of Illinois. The eastern pylon of the Eads Bridge is the southernmost tip of what once was Bloody Island.

The island was so named because it was in neither Illinois nor Missouri, so it was well suited for duels among gentlemen of the day. The most famous duel to (almost) take place there was on September 22, 1842, between

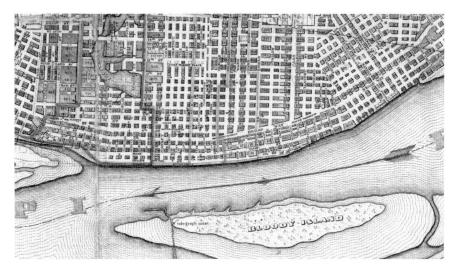

An October 1837 surveyor's map of Bloody Island. *National Parks System*.

Abraham Lincoln and political rival James Shields. It is an intriguing tale but too long to tell here. Ultimately, the two men squared off with swords, but at the last minute they came to a peaceful settlement.

Incidentally, Bloody Island was problematic during this era because the shifting soil caused the island to grow and the channel to narrow, posing a problem for shipping and navigation. Five years before Lincoln's duel, in October 1837, the U.S. Army Corps of Engineers sent a lieutenant engineering officer, Robert E. Lee, to conduct a survey of the island. Lee, of course, later became commander of the Confederate forces during the Civil War.

Let's return to 1850. On October 7, the connection across the Mississippi was completed, and the telegraphic equipment was shipped across the river to St. Louis. The submerged cables functioned far better than suspended ones used in previous attempts. In the summer and fall, work began on the continued expansion of the telegraph to St. Joseph. This turned out to be an ideal location, because the Pikes Peak Stables in St. Joseph was the eastern end of the Pony Express. The much-romanticized Pony Express operated from April 1860 to October 1861—a mere eighteen months—before it closed (see chapter "Neither Snow nor Rain").

During the same period, a telegraph line was created from Cincinnati to St. Louis through Indiana. In 1851, a gutta-percha cable made "upon a new principle" (undoubtedly an improved version) was laid across the Mississippi. Two more lines were laid above Bissell's Ferry.

Abraham Lincoln and political rival James Shields. *Library of Congress*.

Technology advanced rapidly in this era. Only twenty-four years after the submarine cable was laid, in 1874, the Eads Bridge was completed, and, eventually, telegraph wires (followed by telephone and electrical wires) were added to the structure. But twenty-three years after being completed, the bridge was struck during the Great Cyclone of 1896, crushing the eastern section of the bridge and destroying the telegraph wires.

BLOODY ISLAND, EAST ST. LOUIS, ILLINOIS 62201

BREWERS AND THEIR CAVES

F rom early on, St. Louis was known for its breweries. Immigrating Europeans, in particular the Germans, brought with them their love of—and knowledge of how to brew—beer. A great deal has been written about the major brewers, so they will not be covered here.

It is claimed that no other city has more caves beneath it than St. Louis, which has approximately fifty. Today, they are mostly paved over or otherwise made inaccessible, but in the 1800s, they were highly prized by breweries for cold storage and lagering beer. So important were they that brewers sought out the caves and then built their breweries on top of or near them. This includes two of the city's largest brewers, Anheuser-Busch (the cave was discovered in 1852) and Lemp (the Cherokee Cave at Broadway and Cherokee Street, discovered in 1840).

One of the most important (and surprisingly least remembered) brewer caves is Uhrig's Cave, at the intersection of Jefferson and Washington. It has an incredible past. In 1852, it was one of the city's hottest spots. It all began when a Bavarian brewer named Franz Joseph Uhrig, who owned a facility called the Camp Springs Brewery (later just the Uhrig Brewery) on Market Street, purchased the spot because it had a large cave, ideal for the brewing process. Like Lemp, Uhrig expanded the caverns, digging to connect the four large caverns and bricking up parts to minimize seepage. To make the transportation of beer easier, Uhrig built a narrow-gauge railroad between the cave and the factory on Market.

The Civil War interrupted activity briefly, and the cave served as headquarters for the local militia. Later, Uhrig got the great idea of combining

Uhrig's Cave and Brewery, once the coolest place in town, 1870. *Missouri Historical Society*.

cool beer with entertainment, and the cave became far more than a beer storage facility. He built an entertainment venue above ground for music, song and dance. It had its own opera company and a seating capacity of three hundred. It was popularly referred to simply as "The Cave," and local artists were able to put on the popular operettas of Gilbert and Sullivan.

After its popularity waned, the beer garden eventually closed, and in 1908, the location became the site of the massive, three-story St. Louis Coliseum—at the time the largest public building in the country and among the largest in the world. It held fourteen thousand spectators and could expand to hold twenty thousand.

The coliseum was so vast and seated so many people that it quickly replaced the St. Louis Exposition and Music Hall as St. Louis' main indoor arena.

The oval arena was fifty thousand square feet and was suitable for innumerable events, including horse shows and the 1916 Democratic National Convention. In 1925, a six-hundred-thousand-gallon swimming pool was built. Incredibly, the arena's life span was brief—only thirty years— and it was closed in 1939. During World War II, the empty building was used as storage to hold vehicles for the U.S. military.

Another of the old brewer caves is interesting because of its recent rediscovery. English Cave, in the Benton Park neighborhood, was named after Ezra English, a St. Louis ale brewer who made the famous "Double X" ale. In the 1840s, the cave was used not only for refrigerated storage but also as an underground beer garden and entertainment complex. It seated as many as one hundred guests in fifty-five-degree temperatures when it was one hundred degrees above ground.

The cave went through a series of failed businesses: the brewery, a mushroom farm in 1887, then a wine company. It was last used in 1919, after which the entrances were sealed and the area above it was vacant. The exact location fell into obscurity and remained unknown for one hundred years, but it was said to run from Benton Park to the Lemp Brewery, three blocks south and four blocks east. In 2020, local residents and cave enthusiasts pulled together resources to search for the lost cave, and on March 12, they conducted a drilling and lidar expedition and located the lost cave.

Today you can see the drilling site at the English Cave Community Garden on Provenchere Place. And finding the garden down the narrow little street and bricked alleys is half the fun!

The saga of the numerous other breweries is a snapshot of American economics. The dozens of excellent breweries in those early days—Lemp, Fallstaff, Columbia, Otto Stiefel Brewery, Forest Park Brewery, Consumer's Brewery Brew House—were faced with choices of innovating and investing in automation or sticking with the old ways. Those that could not afford improvements to efficiency (or wanted to cling to traditional methods) simply could not compete, and they eventually had to sell out to others.

A lot of people are familiar with the tragic story of the Lemp family and brewery, but to summarize, as a final act, William Lemp Jr. closed his brewery in 1920 and sold the Falstaff brand to his friend Joe Griesedieck before committing suicide in 1922.

Griesedieck planned to buy up failing breweries, including four in St. Louis. Over time, this proved to be a failed strategy, since these breweries were older and the cost of making improvements was too high to compete with Anheuser-Busch. Over time, the plants closed. All that remains are a handful of shells and repurposed properties—and one giant smokestack.

UHRIG'S CAVE, JEFFERSON AVENUE AND WASHINGTON BOULEVARD, ST. LOUIS, MISSOURI 63103
ENGLISH CAVE, 1960 PROVENCHERE PLACE, ST. LOUIS, MISSOURI 63118

THE BRITISH CROWN JEWELS AND THE FIRST POLICE DEPARTMENT TO USE FINGERPRINTS

*A*mong the many splendors of the 1904 World's Fair were the British crown jewels, sent by ship by Queen Victoria. These and innumerable other priceless items were displayed during the fair. With almost twenty million visitors, the potential for theft was a very real possibility. The St. Louis Metropolitan Police Department had 1,260 officers on duty, and other officers were brought in just for the fair. They assumed, correctly, that among fairgoers would be countless pickpockets, swindlers and thieves looking for easy pickings—and for big scores, such as the crown jewels.

The British sent a security team to escort the crown jewels, headed by Sergeant John Kenneth Ferrier of Scotland Yard. Ferrier was there not only to protect the jewels but also to be an exhibitor. He was one of three men with booths in the Education Building, not far from where the crown jewels were displayed, to demonstrate modern techniques of criminal identification. He demonstrated the friction ridge skin (fingerprint) method, as did Captain James J. Parke from New York. Emerson E. Davis from New York demonstrated the "Bertillon Indexer" anthropometric method. (This early identification method, developed by Frenchman Alphonse Bertillon, classified people by four measurements of their body; the system proved much less reliable than fingerprinting. Bertillon was also the inventor of the mug shot.)

The opening day of the fair, May 1, 1904, is said to be the first public display of fingerprinting in the world. That said, the study and application

St. Louis Police using the fingerprint system, 1910. *Missouri Historical Society.*

of fingerprint identification was nothing new. Englishman Sir William James Herschel is credited as the first person to study friction ridge skin, in 1858. Numerous other Europeans studied the distinctive nature of the ridges on the hands, and before 1900, there were many instances of fingerprints being used in cases resulting in conviction.

Other police departments in the United States were evaluating the system. Another police exhibitor during the fair, Captain Parke, was demonstrating the process. So, while still exploratory, the method was by no means unknown. In fact, Mark Twain was the first American writer to incorporate fingerprinting for solving crime in *Life on the Mississippi* in 1883, twenty years earlier.

During his stay in the United States, Ferrier demonstrated the British technique, the Henry system, to officials from Leavenworth and St. Louis. The system, named after Sir Edward Richard Henry, was a scientific filing system based on alphanumeric fingerprint identification and cataloguing. He also demonstrated the techniques to Mary E. Holland and her husband, Phil. She ran the Holland Detective Agency in Chicago and was friends with famous Scottish American detective Allan J. Pinkerton of the Pinkerton National Detective Agency. She became an ardent advocate for fingerprint identification and was once called "the most noted woman criminologist in the world."

Before the fair was even over, in October 1904, the St. Louis Metropolitan Police Department became the first in the nation to set up a fingerprint bureau.

THE BROWN SHOE COMPANY

*D*uring the early twentieth century, St. Louis was one of the largest shoe manufacturing cities in the United States, leading to the expression "famous for shoes, blues and booze."

Several companies exchanged the title of "biggest" over the years, including Buster Brown, International Shoe Company and Samuels Shoe Company. The title was also owned by the Hamilton-Brown Shoe Company, or Brown Shoe.

Founded in 1875, the Brown Shoe Company battled well-established New England shoe companies by producing less-expensive shoes (due to cheaper Midwest labor), which enabled them to gain market share. By 1902, Brown Shoe had five factories operating in St. Louis. In 1904, the firm built the still-surviving Homes-Take Factory on Russell Boulevard.

As machinery improved efficiencies and reduced costs, Brown had to start curbing costs to remain competitive. This naturally meant lower wages. One method was to hire more women and children, who could be paid less.

By 1911, and during the Great Depression, more than half of workers were ages fourteen to nineteen, with weekly wages for a sixteen-year-old girl less than ten dollars. Many people worked as many as sixty hours a week. Low wages and poor conditions led to unions forming, which Brown Shoe vigorously opposed. In one instance, a union rep was nearly tarred and feathered, and government investigators intervened. Eventually, pay improved.

The Brown Shoe exhibit at the 1904 World's Fair. *Missouri Historical Society*.

The International Hat warehouse at 1201 Russell. It became the Homes-Take Factory.

With mounting costs and fewer shoes being purchased during the Depression, in June 1939, the company went bankrupt and the factory was mothballed.

In 1954, the Homes-Take Factory was converted into a warehouse by the International Hat Company, and in 1980, the building became a senior and disabled living facility.

There is some deliberation about the following, but I am going to toss it out there. Until 1850 (some sources say 1818), shoes were made "straight," meaning that there was no differentiation between left and right shoes. Brown Shoe was one of the first companies to make left and right shoes, and it was the first to create different shoes for men and women. However, there are conflicting dates and claims, including the claim that the first pair of right- and left-footed shoes was made in Philadelphia.

As a bit of local trivia, famed playwright Tennessee Williams used to work in the factory when it was International Shoe (his father was an executive there).

Another tidbit is that the ten-story International Shoe building at 750 North Sixteenth Street went on to become the City Museum. This fanciful place features works by local creative genius Bob Cassilly. Visitors are enchanted by the giant praying mantis and school bus on the roof, the jet plane and the snake fence.

1201 RUSSELL BOULEVARD, SOULARD, MISSOURI 63104
CITY MUSEUM, 750 NORTH SIXTEENTH STREET, ST. LOUIS, MISSOURI 63103

CARY GRANT STARTS A TREND

Chocolates on a Hotel Pillow

The Mayfair Hotel (now the Magnolia Hotel), where Cary Grant placed the first chocolate on a hotel pillow.

*D*uring the classic big-screen era, Hollywood stars would stay in the posh Mayfair Hotel in downtown St. Louis when traveling between the coasts. In the 1950s, the famously suave actor Cary Grant and a female companion booked the penthouse suite, and he laid out a trail of chocolates leading to the bedroom. The hotel manager thought it was so romantic that he began the practice of putting chocolates or mints on all the pillows. The practice was soon picked up by luxury hotels everywhere.

The Mayfield went through many renovations and changed hands over the years. It is now the Magnolia Hotel, and you can rent the penthouse suite, which includes one king bed and two guest beds, for $3,650 a night. For that much money, you would think the two guests came with the room.

MAYFAIR HOTEL, 806 ST. CHARLES STREET, ST. LOUIS, MISSOURI 63101

CHINATOWN

Hop Alley and a President's Grandfather

Chinese workers began arriving in St. Louis in 1869, and by 1900, there were somewhere between three hundred and four hundred Chinese immigrants in town. Many migrated to St. Louis from other areas of the country to work in the mines; others worked in factories and laundries and in other unskilled trades.

As the population grew, they were the object of discriminatory housing ordinances that required them to live within one square block, known as Hop Alley, bordered by Market, Seventh, Walnut and Eighth Streets.

Life for Chinese immigrants was as difficult as for most other nonwhite races, and there was a great deal of racial inequality. For example, in 1854, the California Supreme Court ruled that Chinese persons were prohibited from testifying against white Americans in court (*People v. Hall*). The decision was based on the theory that "Native Americans had crossed over to the Americas via the Bering Straits Land Bridge, and thus were descended from Asians, and because Native Americans were lesser humans, by extension then Chinese were lesser humans as well."

Overall, local sentiment toward the Chinese was not positive. Newspapers depicted Hop Alley as a den of criminals, gamblers and opium addicts. In reality, there *was* in fact a severe opium problem—but not among the Chinese population.

In 1895, about 0.5 percent of the nation's population (an astonishing 3.15 million people) was addicted to opium. (Recall that the original formula for Coca-Cola included cocaine.) In this era, the typical American opiate addict was an upper- or middle-class white woman.

The Oriental Tea and Mercantile Company at 22 South Eighth Street in the Chinatown district, 1964. *Missouri Historical Society.*

The primary drug lord of the day was none other than the British Empire. Because of their love of tea, the British had developed a massive trade deficit with China. To resolve this issue, Britain gained a monopoly on opium from India, which British merchants smuggled into China (where it was illegal)—about 900 tons a year in 1800. By 1838, this amount had increased to 1,400 tons. The British fought the two Opium Wars (the first in 1839–42 and the second in 1856–60, aided by the French), which secured lucrative trade deals for silk, porcelain and tea in exchange for silver. By the end of the nineteenth century, roughly one-third of China's population of three hundred million was addicted to opium.

In America, the U.S. Army kicked off the initial domestic tidal wave of opium, issuing ten million opium tablets to solders during the Civil War. In 1890, opiates were sold unregulated, and doctors recommended its use for everything from menstrual cramps to a woman's "nervous character." By the 1860s, women accounted for 60 percent of opium addicts. It wasn't until the 1870s that smoking opium, brought over by the Chinese for recreational use, began spreading in the American West.

This met with great alarm, and President Theodore Roosevelt called for an international opium commission to meet in Shanghai, leading the United States to pass the Opium Exclusion Act in 1909.

This is somewhat ironic, considering our nation played such a large role in addicting the country of China. An American merchant named Warren Delano Jr., the grandfather of future president Franklin Delano Roosevelt, made his fortune smuggling illegal opium from Turkey into China. America's first multimillionaire, John Jacob Astor, also got rich by smuggling opium. Owner of the Astor Fur Company, he sold the Missouri River rights to Pierre Chouteau Jr. in 1838. The Chouteau family, and Auguste Chouteau specifically, is credited with founding St. Louis.

While Hop Alley was not without its issues, the mainstream concepts about the Chinese were wild stereotypes involving crime and opium dens where people got "hopped up" on opium. The reality was that the vast majority of addicts received their opium from their doctors or pharmacists or, during the Civil War, the army. And the supply was brought to them by British and American giants of industry. Yet the Chinese got the blame.

MARKET AND SEVENTH STREETS, ST. LOUIS, MISSOURI 63101

CHOKING ON PROGRESS

The Worst Air Pollution in the Nation

*I*n St. Louis, November 28, 1939, was dubbed "Black Tuesday" because the emissions from factories burning coal were so horrible that one could barely see, in broad daylight, let alone breathe.

St. Louis was a major industrial city, and most of the plants operated coal-burning systems; almost all of these factories used cheap, high-sulfur "soft" (bituminous) coal from nearby mines in Illinois; the closest cleaner-burning "hard" anthracite coal was in Arkansas and cost much more. In 1936, the problem had become so horrific that the mayor appointed Raymond R. Tucker as smoke commissioner to deal with the problem. In 1937, a smoke ordinance was passed with requirements designed to reduce effluent. Businesses and homes were required to use a stoker or to buy washed coal. This is coal that has been mechanically washed to remove impurities such as ash and soil. While more expensive, it produces more energy and reduces effluent. The ordinance also spurred the use of natural gas.

The smoke commissioner ultimately called for a complete ban on the use of soft coal. Industry fought the measure tenaciously; the president of the Illinois United Mine Workers, Ray Edmundson, called the ban "a treasonable act," but the ban was eventually instituted in 1940. While St. Louis businesses and residents were not able to burn the cheaper soft coal legally, there were cases of bootleg cheap coal being purchased illegally. The result of the reform efforts was almost immediate; air became significantly

View of the Civil Courts Building while smoke pollution blots out the sun at midday. *Missouri Historical Society.*

clearer. By 1946, the city had reduced coal smoke by 75 percent. Over the years, even hard coal has been replaced by hydroelectric and other energy sources in an effort to reduce our impact on the environment.

CHOLERA OUTBREAK OF 1849
KILLS 10 PERCENT OF POPULATION

*F*rom the time of its earliest settlement by Europeans, the area now occupied by St. Louis had no large lakes. But in 1766, Joseph Taillon dammed La Petite Rivière (Mill Creek) to power the waterwheel of his gristmill. In so doing, he changed the landscape massively, creating a one-hundred-acre lake in the middle of town.

In 1779, the famous local figure Auguste Chouteau purchased the lake, thereafter known as Chouteau's Pond. Locals apparently loved the idyllic setting, wildlife and serenity the pond brought.

By the 1830s, the land around the lake had been bought up by businesses and factories, and soon it was transformed from idyllic to horrific. By the mid-1840s, the lake had become a cesspool of pollution. Industrial and human waste were pervasive throughout the city: "The pond proved a convenient dumping ground for the rotting garbage of butcher shops, flour mills, and hide tanneries."

The largely stagnant, rancid waters proved to be the ideal breeding ground for cholera. In 1849, cholera swept through the city, killing 10 percent of the population. Hundreds of victims who had succumbed to the disease were simply buried, thrown in the river or dumped on carts that traveled the streets at night picking up bodies.

A few years before the outbreak (1842), City Engineer Henry Kayser chose the cheapest way of getting rid of wastewater. He simply ran it into the limestone caves running beneath the city. Eventually, the folly of the design became apparent when a sinkhole developed and flooded an area at Biddle

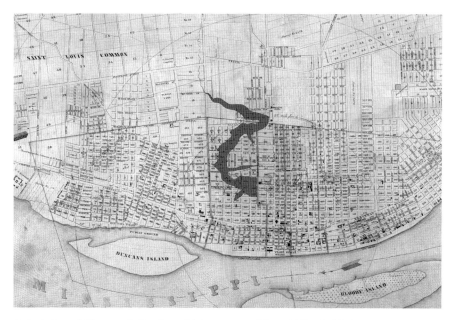

A depiction of Chouteau's Pond overlaid on a map. *Missouri Historical Society*.

View of St. Louis from the south side of beautiful Chouteau's Pond, 1891. *Missouri Historical Society*.

and Tenth Streets (currently occupied by an assisted living center northwest of the America's Center), earning the burning nickname "Kayser's Lake."

Amid the epidemic, the putrid Chouteau's Pond was identified as a key cause of the disease, and doctors demanded the lake be drained.

After the area was drained, the reclaimed land was sold and used for many other purposes. Much of it became part of Union Station's rail yards, near the area that is now home to the St. Louis Aquarium. Tracing the evolution, the area went from farmland to lake to industrial center to sewer to rail yards and back to the water as the aquarium.

CIVIL WAR CONTRABAND HOSPITALS AND BLACK HEALTHCARE

*P*rior to emancipation, slaves had almost no access to professional medical care. They mostly practiced medicine brought from their homelands.

As the Civil War was drawing to a close, more and more Blacks fled the war-torn South. Droves of people marched north, and in short order the Union army had an unexpected problem: how to house, feed and provide medical care for hundreds of thousands of refugees.

The ugly reality is that Union major general Benjamin Butler, in assessing the difficulty, classified Blacks, legally, as confiscated enemy property. That is, the U.S. Army officially referred to them as "contraband," in the same way it would a confiscated wagon or team of horses.

As such, the federal government did not build "Refugee Camps"; instead, they built "Contraband Camps." The National Library of Medicine notes that the first location to provide medical care to freed Blacks was the Bethesda Maryland Contraband Hospital. This location continued its care and education of Black people, and in 1975, it became Howard University Hospital.

The first Contraband Camp in St. Louis is not where you would expect— the Missouri Hotel. The hotel is also where the first legislature convened under the first state constitution on September 18, 1820. This was a year before Missouri was admitted to the Union. Refugees stayed there temporarily until moved to Benton Barracks (located at Fairground Park). Sadly, hundreds of people died there of smallpox.

City Hospital No. 2, Barnes Medical College, Lawton Boulevard, 1920. *Missouri Historical Society.*

This hotel was on the corner of Main Street (later renamed First Street) and Morgan Street and is now the location of the Raeder Building. You are perhaps more acquainted with its current tenant, the Old Spaghetti Factory on Laclede's Landing.

The following years were highly unstable as African Americans integrated into northern society. There was little appreciable advancement in medical care for years. Care was usually available only in the segregated units of the public hospitals, and the for-profit model made almost all treatment out of reach financially for Black families.

It wasn't until 1919 that a dedicated medical facility was established, City Hospital No. 2, which had changed hands numerous times in the previous years. It began life as the Barnes Medical College for instruction of white doctors. The five-story building stood on the northeast corner of Lawton (now Chestnut Street) and Garrison.

Built in 1892, the college had outworn its usefulness and was sold or underwent several changes over the next few years in rapid succession. At least part of the facility became the Douglass Hotel (for Black residents). Records are incomplete, sketchy or conflicting, but the building then became Centenary Hospital. It was later purchased by Christian Hospital. There is one reference that the facility may have been abandoned at one point.

In 1918, the city was pressured to develop a hospital to provide care for Black residents, and it purchased the dilapidated college. It was small (only 177 beds), old and ill-equipped. It was such a hazard that the Black doctors nicknamed it "the firetrap." In 1930, a Black physician was electrocuted while using a defective X-ray machine.

It was so overcrowded that staff often had to tie two beds together to accommodate three or more patients. The facility was by all measures wholly inadequate. But it was the only option for care through 1937. It was one of only three hospitals in St. Louis City that served Black patients.

In 1937, after struggling since 1914 to achieve reasonable medical care for African Americans, the city finally built Homer G. Phillips Hospital. It was the first teaching hospital west of the Mississippi to serve Blacks and was the city's only Black hospital until 1979.

Homer G. Phillips Hospital, 1938. *Missouri Historical Society.*

For twenty years, 75 percent of all Black doctors in the country interned there. By 1961, it had trained the largest number of Black doctors and nurses in the world.

Phillips was ranked among the ten largest hospitals in the country and was one of only two institutions where Black doctors could go for training. It could accommodate six hundred patients and had a five-story nurse's building for training, housing students and classrooms.

While filling a critical niche for St. Louis, the hospital battled to retain solvency, competing for tax dollars with other facilities. It operated until it closed in 1979, at which point other hospitals were prohibited from discriminating in delivering medical care or segregating patients. Note that hospitals largely did not do so until required by law.

In 2003, the facility reopened as the Homer G. Phillips Dignity House/ Senior Living Community.

MISSOURI HOTEL, MAIN STREET (FIRST STREET) AND MORGAN STREET, ST. LOUIS, MISSOURI 63102

HOMER G. PHILLIPS HOSPITAL, 2601 NORTH WHITTIER STREET, ST. LOUIS, MISSOURI 63113

CIVIL WAR IRONCLADS
OF JAMES EADS

*A*t the outbreak of the Civil War, the federal government asked engineer James Eads his advice for gaining control of the lower Mississippi. He recommended building a fleet of ironclad vessels, which would be largely impervious to the artillery of the day. These vessels would enable the Union to maintain a stranglehold on southern passage along the Mississippi, inhibiting both trade and troop movement.

The government issued Eads contracts for seven ironclad gunboats, which were completed within one hundred days. From 1861 to 1864, he built a total of thirteen at two St. Louis ironworks: the Union Marine Works in Carondelet, Missouri (aka Union Iron Works) and the Mound City Marine Railway and Shipyard in Mound City, Illinois. The Union Marine Works was located at the end of Davis Street, north of Jefferson Barracks at the confluence of the River Des Peres and the Mississippi River.

The ironclads devastated the Confederate economy and greatly impaired river traffic for the South's transport of food, finished goods and troops.

A historical marker referencing the ironclads is located in Bellerive Park at the corner of South Broadway and Baker Streets. Another tribute to Eads and his ironclads is found at South St. Louis Square Park, where the James Eads Memorial Cannon stands with a plaque. (This is a concrete replica of a cannon made from a mold of an actual ironclad cannon.)

The salvaged remains of one of seven shallow-draft City Class river ironclads, the USS *Cairo* (named after the town in Illinois, not Egypt), built by Eads at Mound City Marine, commissioned in January 1862, can be

USS *Cairo*, Union gunboat, 1863. It was sunk by a mine during the war and later brought up. It is on display at the Vicksburg National Military Park in Vicksburg, Mississippi. *Missouri Historical Society*.

The James Eads Memorial Cannon (concrete) in South St. Louis Square Park, 2020.

viewed at Vicksburg National Military Park in Vicksburg, Mississippi. It was the first ship to be sunk by a mine.

Following the war, the Union Iron Works was used to fabricate the caissons used during construction of the Eads Bridge (1869–70).

BELLERIVE PARK, 5570 SOUTH BROADWAY, ST. LOUIS, MISSOURI 63111
ST. LOUIS SQUARE PARK, 7701 SOUTH BROADWAY, ST. LOUIS, MISSOURI 63111

COFFEE WAS KING

St. Louis used to be one of the most important coffee hubs in the nation and arguably the world long before Starbucks. In 1845, the St. Louis City Directory listed over fifty coffeehouses (the total population at the time was thirty-five thousand people). From 1900 to 1920, St. Louis was the largest inland distributor of coffee in the world, with around eighty different coffee roasters in the area.

The claim for being the first company to sell roasted coffee west of the Mississippi is made by the James H. Forbes Tea & Coffee Company, in 1853, eight years before the Civil War. Forbes was located at 112 Locust Street, which today appears to be dead center under the Gateway Arch. In 1910, it moved to a five-story building at 908 Clark Street. That building was torn down in 1963. You've probably driven right over the spot: the onramp for I-64.

At least one source states that the largest and oldest coffee company is… Ronnoco? But that doesn't seem to pan out. More than one account tells how the two founding brothers (named O'Connor) witnessed coffee being roasted at the 1904 World's Fair and decided to start making their own. Ronnoco's own website states that the brothers "experienced an innovation that changed their lives at the 1904 World's Fair in St. Louis—imported coffee beans roasted over a gas flame."

In fact, the O'Connor brothers did not even form Ronnoco until 1919 (the name *Ronnoco*, incidentally, is *O'Connor* spelled backward). To tell you how long ago this was, they delivered coffee beans to local hotels by horse-drawn buggy.

Above: Blanke Coffee Pavilion on the 1904 World's Fair grounds, 1904. *Missouri Historical Society*.

Opposite: Ulysses S. Grant residence "Hardscrabble." *Missouri Historical Society*.

So who was the inspiration that the O'Connor brothers saw? One of the many other early coffee companies was Faust Coffee. (Faust is a character out of German legend, Johann Faust, who made a pact with the devil. I am not sure why this was a good marketing scheme, but you can't say it isn't memorable.)

Faust Coffee was owned by a man named Cyrus F. Blanke. He secured contracts with the railroads and captured a nationwide market. Blanke claimed to have the largest coffee-roasting plant in the world, located in a beautiful building (still around today) on Fourteenth Street.

Blanke was actually *selling* coffee at the 1904 World's Fair. It is possible that his was the coffee that the O'Connors saw. In a marketing brainstorm, for the fair, Blanke purchased the cabin of Ulysses S. Grant for $8,000 and moved it to Forest Park, where the fair was held. (Grant's wife, Julia, disliked the crude cabin so much she nicknamed it "Hardscrabble.")

Somehow, Blanke obtained permission to have the cabin re-assembled in a prime location, at the east wing of the Palace of Arts. That building is one

of the only buildings from the World's Fair still standing today and is now known as the St. Louis Art Museum.

He put Grant's cabin east of the palace. And what now stands east of the Art Museum? The new wing of the museum, which houses the Panorama restaurant. Today, you can go to the same location and buy yourself a cup of coffee.

In 1907, Blanke sold Grant's cabin to August Busch, who moved it close to its original location in Grant's Farm. Today, there are about twenty different coffee roasters in the St. Louis area. Bonus fact: Comet Coffee within the Highlands (across from Forest Park, south of I-64) is built on the location of the Comet rollercoaster (see chapter "Forest Park Highlands and the St. Louis Carousel").

BLANKE BUILDING, 904 SOUTH FOURTEENTH STREET, ST. LOUIS, MISSOURI 63103
GRANT'S FARM, 10501 GRAVOIS ROAD, ST. LOUIS, MISSOURI 63123

CONGRESSMAN BEATEN ON SENATE FLOOR AND THE FIRST BLACK HIGH SCHOOL WEST OF THE MISSISSIPPI

*O*n May 22, 1856, Representative Preston Brooks of South Carolina entered the Senate and repeatedly beat Massachusetts senator Charles Sumner in the head with a gold-topped walking stick—so hard, in fact, that the cane broke. Sumner's injuries were so severe that he was unable to return to the Senate until 1859. He would go on to have his name on the first Black high school west of the Mississippi.

The event originated as the anger between the North and South was reaching crisis level. Sumner's beating in 1856, in fact, was over an abolitionist speech he gave. Nine years before the assault, in 1847, the Missouri legislature banned education for free Blacks. It was yet another contributing factor to the friction that ultimately brought the country to war from 1861 to 1865.

A decade after the war ended, in 1875, St. Louis opened Sumner School, the first school for Blacks west of the Mississippi. But not in the Ville, where you would presume it to be located.

It first opened at Eleventh Street between Poplar and Spruce. This was the location of the old Washington Elementary School (not to be confused with the Washington/Euclid School), a whites-only school that had become so dilapidated it was deemed unfit and had been abandoned. The property was for sale for six months with no offers until it was picked up for educating Black children.

It was a de facto practice for Blacks to inherit facilities like schools and hospitals that were deemed no longer suitable for the white populace (see

SOUTHERN CHIVALRY — ARGUMENTversus CLUB'S.

"Southern Chivalry." A period illustration showing Preston Brooks beating Charles Sumner's head like a piñata, resulting in a three-year absence for Sumner from the Senate. *Wikipedia Commons*.

chapter "Civil War Contraband Hospitals and Black Healthcare"). The school originally was a combined elementary and high school, and almost half of the city's Black students attended there.

The location of the original Sumner School was once underwater—within the boundary of Chouteau's Pond. This was a man-made lake in the middle of St. Louis created in the early 1800s by damming up Mill Creek (then an open sewer). It became incredibly polluted and was responsible for a cholera outbreak in 1849 that killed 10 percent of the city's population (see chapter "Cholera Outbreak of 1849 Kills 10 Percent of Population").

Note also that the Collier White Lead Works was across the street from Washington Elementary. Another problem was that the school was across the street from the old Four Courts Building at Twelfth (now Tucker) and Clark, which included police headquarters, the city morgue, the city jail and criminal and police courts. Children had to walk past the city gallows and morgue on the way to school.

In 1896, the school moved to Fifteenth and Walnut for three years and reopened in 1909 in a beautiful, new building in its current location (4248 Cottage Avenue). Unlike most previous facilities, the new Sumner High School was a purpose-built, state-of-the-art facility with a Georgian Revival

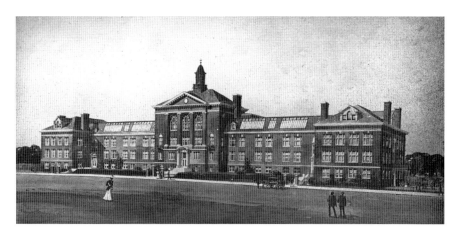

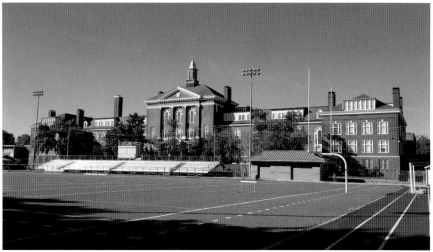

Top: Sumner High School, 1904. *Missouri Historical Society*.

Bottom: Sumner High School, 2020.

edifice. It was the first high school for Black students west of the Mississippi. Located just a block from where the marvelous Homer G. Phillips Hospital stood, it was part of a thriving Black neighborhood. Although a segregated facility, it was the closest St. Louis would come to "separate but equal."

SUMNER HIGH SCHOOL, 4248 COTTAGE AVENUE, ST. LOUIS, MISSOURI 63113

DANIEL BOONE'S REAL HOME

*T*he St. Louis region has a legitimate albeit exaggerated connection to pioneer Daniel Boone. Much is made of the Historic Daniel Boone Home in Defiance, Missouri (west of St. Louis), yet the name is misleading. Instead, the location of the cabin built by Boone is in Overland (on the corner of Wabaday and Kenosho, next to Wyland Elementary School). Boone built the one-room cabin in 1799 as a leaping-off point for the Overland Trail. The cabin was demolished in 1880.

Back to the fanciful legend. The Historic Daniel Boone Home was built by, owned and occupied by Boone's youngest son, Nathaniel. But Daniel did live his last few years there and died there on September 26, 1820. The operators of the site hesitantly divulge that there is little evidence that Boone spent time on the property other than this.

A marker commemorates the location of Daniel Boone's 1799 cabin at the corner of Wabaday and Kenosho, 2020.

The myth is exacerbated as well by the tale of the "judgement tree." This territory was originally claimed by the Spanish, and Boone was hired as a sort of traveling judge. The story goes that he tried cases beneath this tree. Today, there is no tree, only a concrete casting of a downed tree where a tree once stood. And there is conflicting evidence of this being the location of the tree. There were apparently two such trees. And there is a Judgement Tree Memorial located on Highway 94 near the Katy Trail in nearby Matson.

All this said, the place name is wholly misleading, yet it has been placed in the National Register of Historic Places, and the owners have invested millions in recreating a period village. So they aren't interested in revising the legend.

DANIEL BOONE'S CABIN (MARKER), WABADAY AND KENOSHO AVENUES,
    ST. LOUIS, MISSOURI 63114

DENYING THE VOTE

*T*here is an old Russian quote (in all likelihood misattributed to Joseph Stalin): "It's not the people who vote that count, it's the people who count the votes."

In the earliest years of this nation, the right to vote was limited to white, male property owners. Many states administered literacy tests to exclude "undesirables" from voting, and some states even administered religion tests to exclude non-Christians. Over time, some of the rules were relaxed or eliminated, but for decades, huge segments of the American populace were excluded from exercising the right to vote.

Right after the Civil War, millions of former slaves were granted citizenship when Congress passed the Fourteenth Amendment in June 1866, granting them "equal protection of the laws." However, it had loopholes that enabled states to deny Blacks the right to vote.

To circumvent the Fourteenth Amendment, in 1865–66, most southern states enacted "Black Codes," which prevented African Americans from voting. This was viewed as imperative, because given an equal voice, Blacks would institute legislation that would provide them equal citizenship—the opposite of what established society desired. An article in the *Henderson Gold Leaf* newspaper (in Henderson, North Carolina) dated May 24, 1900, reads:

Above: Several thousand suffragettes in St. Louis held a silent demonstration, lining both sides of Locust for ten blocks from the Hotel Jefferson to the St. Louis Coliseum on the opening day of the Democratic National Convention, June 14, 1916. *State Historical Society of Missouri.*

Opposite: Demonstrators on the stairs of the old Art Museum, northeast corner of Lucas Place (now Locust Street) and Nineteenth Street. The sign on the wall reads, "Headquarters National State and City Woman's Suffrage Assn. Welcome!" *Missouri Historical Society.*

> *CURSED BY A NEGRO VOTE. The political conditions of the South, especially in States like North Carolina where there is such a large illiterate negro vote, grow worse with each year. It does not take an expert to observe this State of affairs, but the most casual observer easily sees that the negro vote is a curse to our fair Southland and that the only remedy for this evil is the disfranchisement of this ignorant vote.*

To resolve this, in February 1870, Congress passed the Fifteenth Amendment, making it illegal to deny the right to vote on the basis of race. But that still didn't prevent places, especially southern states, from finding ways to block Blacks from voting. Poll taxes were instituted (assessing a fee for voting, when most African Americans could barely afford daily needs). They also returned to literacy tests to exclude a largely illiterate Black population. This proved highly effective since, for example, our own state of Missouri had passed a law in 1847 banning the education of Blacks and "mulattoes." Such laws were enacted with the express purpose of keeping Blacks, immigrants and low-income white people from voting.

It was not until August 1962 that Congress passed yet another amendment, the Twenty-Fourth Amendment, to finally eliminate poll taxes. But it still did not eliminate all the loopholes. The issues were not eradicated until the passage of the Voting Rights Act of 1965, designed to enforce the voting rights of the Fourteenth and Fifteenth Amendments.

This means that for a century, from 1866 to 1965, states successfully sidestepped federal law to deprive Black voters of their rights. But finally, after one hundred years, Black people could finally vote. Well, half of them, anyway. Not Black women. Well, not any women.

The women's suffrage movement began around 1900 and saw slow but gradual advancement. In 1910, the St. Louis Equal Suffrage League was formed. In June 1916, the city held the National Democratic Convention at the St. Louis Coliseum (see chapter "Brewers and Their Caves"). Between two thousand and seven thousand women, depending on the source, held a silent demonstration, lining both sides of Locust Street for ten blocks from Hotel Jefferson to the coliseum. On the convention's opening day, women staged a demonstration on the steps of the old Art Museum on Locust and Nineteenth.

In March 1919, the National Suffrage Association held its convention in St. Louis at the Statler Hotel on Washington Avenue. The Statler was renovated in 2002. Today, you would recognize it by its current name, the Marriott St. Louis Grand Hotel.

Finally, on August 26, 1920, Congress passed the Nineteenth Amendment, giving women the right to vote.

OLD ART MUSEUM, LUCAS PLACE (NOW LOCUST STREET) AND NINETEENTH STREET, 1815 LOCUST STREET, ST. LOUIS, MISSOURI 63103

HOTEL STATLER (MARRIOTT ST. LOUIS GRAND HOTEL), 800 WASHINGTON AVENUE, ST. LOUIS, MISSOURI 63101

DOUBLE-WIDE ALLEY

Remnant of a Clay Mine Railway

T here is a one-block stretch of double-wide alley running parallel to Chippewa Street between Macklind and Brannon Avenues that is a remnant of St. Louis' long history in clay mining and as a premier manufacturer of bricks.

Anyone who has ever lived in St. Louis can attest to the huge amount of brick used in older buildings. The city used to be an epicenter of the brick-firing industry. This was because the factories were built near the source of raw material: clay.

Beneath many parts of town were massive deposits of clay, much of which was a type of clay ideally suited for high-temperature bricks used in furnaces or kilns and in sewer pipes. (Nearby Dogtown has twenty-seven mines and some nineteen miles of clay mines beneath it.)

The *Laclede-Christy No. 2* locomotive, nicknamed the "Dinkey," which resides at the National Museum of Transportation, 2020.

Here is where the alley comes in. It is where a small rail line was built connecting the clay mines to the brick factories of the Laclede-Christy Brick Works. Over time, after the industry largely closed, the rail line was removed, and the corridor was repurposed. The only remaining section is this two-lane paved alley with a center greenway.

A double-lane paved alley running parallel to Chippewa Street between Macklind and Brannon Avenues, 2020.

The locomotive for the line was a 1907 thirty-inch narrow gauge coal burner built by the Davenport Locomotive Works, the *Laclede-Christy No. 2* (informally referred to as "the Dinkey"). You can see the Dinkey today at the National Museum of Transportation here in town. The brick factory disappeared, too. On the site now is the Burlington Coat Factory next to the American Czech Education Center.

DOUBLE ALLEY, 4235 MACKLIND AVENUE, ST. LOUIS, MISSOURI 63109
NATIONAL MUSEUM OF TRANSPORTATION, 2933 BARRETT STATION ROAD, ST.
    LOUIS, MISSOURI 63122

THE DRED AND HARRIET SCOTT CASE

The Old Courthouse

Sculpture of Dred and Harriet Scott at the Old Courthouse, where their case was heard, 2020.

*T*he Dred and Harriet Scott case is one of our nation's most important decisions. It originated here, and the decision was instrumental in plunging our nation into one of the most tumultuous (and deadly) periods in our history.

The St. Louis Courthouse (facing the Gateway Arch) is where Dred and Harriet Scott filed for their freedom. The law they evoked stated that if a slave had entered a free state or was taken to a free territory, he or she was automatically freed. Even if they were to return to a slave state, they could not be re-enslaved.

Initially, Scott won his case, but it moved up through the state and later federal courts and then to the U.S. Supreme Court, where an infamous ruling declared two things: people of African ancestry were not U.S. citizens and thus could not sue in federal court; and the Fifth Amendment protected slave owners' property rights.

Later, the Scotts were sold and eventually freed. Dred Scott worked as a porter at Barnum's Hotel at Second and Walnut Streets in St. Louis (now the Arch grounds), and he died of tuberculosis in 1858. The couple is buried in Calvary Cemetery in St. Louis, but it is hard to find. (Their markers are humble, given their role in history.)

There is an interesting side note: the steps of this very courthouse, just feet from the statue of the Scotts, was the site of slave auctions. The courthouse itself had the first cast-iron dome ever built, in 1862.

OLD COURT HOUSE, 11 NORTH FOURTH STREET, ST. LOUIS, MISSOURI 63102
CALVARY CEMETERY, 5239 WEST FLORISSANT AVENUE, ST. LOUIS,
   MISSOURI 63115

EDUCATION IN ST. LOUIS

*O*ne of the most misunderstood aspects of life in earlier times is the experience of children growing up. In the early days of America, children were viewed as little people, fit to begin a lifetime of work by age eight. Most of them, it was believed, had no need for a formal education. Education was reserved for learning a trade and for moral or religious lessons. It did not involve the three *R*s: reading, 'riting and 'rithmetic.

In early St. Louis, formal education (either in schools or by private tutor) was limited to the elite and wealthy and people in the professional class who needed to read and write to conduct business. Montreal-born Monsieur Jean Baptiste Truteau operated private schools for boys in St. Louis. Truteau (Trudeau) was French Canadian, later a British subject with the British conquest of Canada and then an American following the acquisition of the Louisiana Purchase by the United States. He was from a prestigious family; among his descendants is Justin Trudeau, prime minister of Canada. He was an explorer, trapper, fur trader and surveyor, and he opened a school in St. Louis.

Education was vastly different for girls, focusing on moral instruction, music and domestic skills such as sewing. With few exceptions, society felt there was no need for girls to read or write. One source states that in early America it was not uncommon for girls to be taught to read but not to write. One of the pioneers in teaching girls in this region was Sister Rose Philippine Duchesne, originally from Grenoble. After sailing ten weeks to New Orleans in 1818, she and her fellow nuns took one of the newly

Des Peres School, 6307 Michigan Avenue, site of the nation's first public kindergarten, 1876. *Missouri Historical Society.*

established steamboats upriver to St. Louis and from there to neighboring St. Charles. That year, she established the first free school west of the Mississippi in a log cabin school.

The first public elementary schools in St. Louis were not founded until 1838: the North School, at the northeast corner of Broadway and Martin Luther King Boulevard (then Cherry Street), and South School, located at the southwest corner of Fourth and Spruce Streets. South School was later named Laclede Primary School. Following the Civil War, public education was given a higher social priority. In 1867, the number of public schools in Missouri was 48,000; by 1870, it had increased to 75,000. Enrollment in the same period grew from 169,000 to 280,000 students.

In 1873, St. Louis introduced the nation's first public kindergarten at the Des Peres School, which had forty-two students the first year. Within a decade of the introduction of kindergarten, every public school in St. Louis offered kindergarten classes. Founder Susan Blow came from a prominent St. Louis family; her grandfather was Peter Blow, who gained I am sure unwanted notoriety—he owned Dred Scott, a slave whose case to gain freedom was heard in the Old Courthouse (see chapter "The Dred and Harriet Scott Case"). Blow's two-story brick schoolhouse still stands on Michigan Avenue and houses the Carondelet Historical Society.

In 1855, St. Louis opened its first high school, Central High School, at Fifteenth and Olive. It was one of the first coeducational high schools in the country. But in 1900, only 11 percent of high school–age children were enrolled in school.

In addition to public schools, there were also a considerable number of private schools (mainly religious). The largest private school system in Missouri was the Archdiocese of St. Louis, established in 1886, which administered about seventy Catholic elementary schools with twenty-two thousand students. As time passed, it was apparent that workers needed higher levels of education, and formal education became more of the norm.

The biggest factor affecting education was race. Early on, there were no public schools for Black children; what little education was available was provided at Black churches—that is, until 1847, when Missouri made it illegal to teach Blacks how to read or write. In response, the pastor of the First Baptist Church, John Berry Meachum (whose grave can be found in Bellefontaine Cemetery), created the "Floating Freedom School" on the Mississippi River, where the interstate waterways are governed by federal law and Missouri law could not be enforced.

Des Peres School, 6303 Michigan Avenue, St. Louis, Missouri 63111
Central High School, 801 North Eleventh Street, St. Louis,
    Missouri 63101

ELECTRIC PARK
AT CREVE COEUR PARK

*C*reve Coeur Lake was home to one of the most famous places in the city that you never even knew existed: Electric Park. It was one of the premiere destinations in town, but it was brought to ruin by gangsters.

It all began around 1887, when a local farmer built the first of several hotels, dance pavilions and boathouses on what used to be the Upper Lake. Creve Coeur Lake used to be two lakes, but the smaller lake, Upper Lake, eventually disappeared due to siltation.

Sensing an opportunity, in 1899, the United Railway Company (which later became Bi-State) built a streetcar line from Delmar Gardens (Delmar and Kingsland) to Creve Coeur Park, effectively bringing masses of people from a major city to the countryside.

Investors began developing both the lake area and the hill overlooking the lake, which today is east of Marine north of Dorsett. The road into the park on the hill is called Streetcar Drive, because this is where the streetcars would loop around to make a return trip to the city.

At that location in 1899 the United Railway Company erected a large brick building as a booster station for the electricity that powered the streetcars. The building still stands and is used by the Go Ape! company. Today, the paved road that loops by the building follows the path of the original streetcar line.

Around this loop, many other features sprang up, and it evolved into an amusement park known as Electric Park. Most people have never heard of this place, as few traces of it remain. One remnant is a very long set of

A streetcar at Creve Coeur Lake Memorial Park, site of the Electric Park, 1915. *Missouri Historical Society.*

concrete stairs (219 of them) and sidewalks leading from the old streetcar area on top of the hill to the lake below.

Later, a cable car was added in this area that traveled from the top of the hill to the lakefront. Gravity powered the descent, and a powered cable pulled it back up the hill.

Another feature was the 255-foot DeForest observation tower. It was relocated to Creve Coeur Park from Forest Park, where it had served as a wireless telegraph tower at the 1904 World's Fair. At that time, a transmitter from the tower sent up to five thousand words per day to the *St. Louis Post-Dispatch* and the *St. Louis Star* downtown. Not far from there in the woods you can see concrete pads on which the tower stood.

This is where the story turns sordid. By the 1920s, Electric Park's popularity had begun to wane when Prohibition was enacted; there was a progressive encroachment of "gangsters and hoodlums" into the dance pavilions, restaurants and nightclubs on the lakefront. Prohibition brought illegal liquor and organized crime until, by 1933, Creve Coeur was almost

The DeForest Observation Tower, 1910. It was moved to Creve Coeur Park after the 1904 World's Fair, where it served as a wireless telegraph tower. *Missouri Historical Society.*

exclusively a gangster hideout. There are stories of firearms from this era being recovered from the lake during dredging.

With the repeal of Prohibition, the criminal element eventually faded away, and with it went Electric Park, the observation tower, the cable car and all the lakeside buildings. It has since been revitalized with walking and bicycling paths, picnic areas, a soccer park and recreational watercraft of all sorts.

CREVE COEUR MEMORIAL PARK STAIRCASE, 13450 MARINE AVENUE, ST. LOUIS, MISSOURI 63146

THE ELEPHANT THAT WALKED ACROSS THE EADS BRIDGE

S t. Louis owes its existence to the Mississippi River. Prior to 1874, everything and everyone that arrived here came by boat. Even after the railroads were built all the way to the Illinois side of the river, freight was shipped from the East by rail, and rail cars were ferried across the Mississippi.

During that era, no one believed a bridge could be built across the Mississippi. The cost would be astronomical. But engineer James Eads developed a design based on a bridge built across the Rhine River at Koblenz, Prussia.

Eads's bridge was to become the world's first arched steel truss bridge and came to be considered a top engineering marvel. Before the Gateway Arch, the Eads Bridge was the symbol of St. Louis and westward expansion.

A major engineering challenge was posed. In order to achieve stability and to support the bridge's weight, the foundations had to rest on bedrock. On the St. Louis side, the bedrock was fairly close to the river's bottom, but on the Illinois side, the bedrock was 110 feet below the soil. It would be necessary to find a way to dig through a hundred feet of earth, underwater, and *then* build the piers of the bridge. No wonder it was considered an impossible feat.

To undertake the underwater digging, Eads built steel "pneumatic caissons" (essentially giant watertight metal boxes). They were floated out on the river and submerged, and workers then syphoned out the silt and mud. The weight of the caisson pushed it down, enabling workers to burrow into and displace the silt.

As a publicity stunt, John Robinson led a "test elephant" (from a traveling circus) across the Eads Bridge on June 14, 1874. The myth was that elephants wouldn't walk across unsafe structures.

On shore, large coal-powered stations generated power to pump air down into the caissons and to run the mechanical excavation equipment. Workers dug so deep they began to get what was dubbed "caisson's disease," commonly called "the bends." Doctors eventually determined that workers needed to return to the surface slowly to avoid the condition.

A less-discussed aspect of the bridge's construction was the tunnel under downtown St. Louis. The bridge emerged in the middle of downtown, amid many buildings. To retain the buildings, a 4,880-foot-long tunnel was dug 30 feet below street level, running mainly under public streets, to connect the rail line to Union Station.

There were extensive problems with the tunnel, including soft soil and seepage, and the initial route had to be altered. In addition, smoke from the coal-burning locomotives was unbearable, as a ventilation system was not part of the original design. Locomotive smoke made the platform under the Post Office and Customs House (now the Old Post Office) unusable. An underground smokestack with a giant fan was eventually installed in the middle of the tunnel. Today, the tunnel and Eads Bridge are used by Metrolink, St. Louis' light-rail system.

When the bridge and tunnel neared completion, they needed to be tested. On June 14, 1874, as a publicity stunt, an elephant from a traveling zoo was marched across the bridge. (There was a popular belief that elephants wouldn't cross an unsafe bridge.) Two weeks later, a real test was conducted, with fourteen locomotives running across the bridge at the same time.

The bridge opened on Independence Day 1874. A parade fourteen miles long ran through St. Louis, and 150,000 people watched General William Tecumseh Sherman drive the last spike. In 1964, the National Park Service named the bridge a National Historic Landmark.

ELIZA HOOLE
IS NOT BURIED HERE

Marker placed for Eliza Hoole, often mistaken for a headstone.

*T*ens of thousands of visitors a year stroll through Tower Grove Park and stumble across, of all things, an almost illegible headstone. It is a curious place for a grave, one must imagine. If you look closely, you can read the date: 1882. So, whose headstone is it? It reads:

OAK
ELIZA HOOLE
1882

Here is the kicker: the stone does not mark a grave at all. Eliza Hoole was the cousin of Henry Shaw, beloved St. Louis philanthropist who donated the land for Tower Grove Park and creator of the Missouri Botanical Garden. When Hoole first visited the park, she fell in love with it and donated an oak tree to a beautification program. Henry placed this marker with the tree type, her name and the date. The tree died long ago, but the marker still reveals the location. The marker can be found in the southwest quarter of the park, north of the intersection of Arsenal and Lackland (just south across the West End Site picnic area/lavatory and walking path).

TOWER GROVE PARK, 4257 NORTHEAST DRIVE, ST. LOUIS, MISSOURI 63110

THE EXORCIST HOUSE

*T*he Exorcist House is another piece of obscure and arcane St. Louis history. The story is made famous by the 1973 supernatural thriller *The Exorcist*, and the base story is essentially real. In the film, the story is set in Washington, D.C., and revolves around a twelve-year-old girl, Regan. In actuality, it took place in St. Louis during the spring of 1949, and the child was a thirteen-year-old boy from Maryland named Ronald Hunkeler.

The first clerical intervention started in Maryland. There, the boy had the word "LOUIS" scratched into his chest, after which his parents brought him to St. Louis.

The private residence where some of the 1949 exorcism took place, 2020.

Two Jesuits, Father Walter H. Halloran and Reverend William Bowdern of St. Francis Xavier Church, agreed to conduct the exorcism. In St. Louis, it started in the home of relatives but was subsequently concluded at Saint Louis University and Alexian Brothers Hospital. After several months, during the last phase of the exorcism, one night during one of Ronald's rages, staff put relics on his chest. Minutes later, he came out of his trance and simply said, "He's gone." The room was sealed off after the exorcism, and that wing of Alexian Brothers Hospital was demolished in 1978, replaced by St. Alexius Hospital.

ALEXIAN BROTHERS HOSPITAL, 3933 SOUTH BROADWAY, ST. LOUIS, MISSOURI 63118

FAIRGROUND PARK AND THE 1949 SWIMMING POOL RACE RIOT

*O*ne of St. Louis' more curious places is Fairground Park. The park was a destination/attraction and was home to the city's first zoo. Along with horseracing, it had monkeys, llamas, antelopes, tapirs, buffalo, leopards, bears and a warthog. Admission was twenty-five cents for adults and ten cents for children. During the Civil War, it was commandeered by the Union army and became Benton Barracks.

The racetrack was a primary source of the park's revenue, but in 1905, right after the World's Fair, betting on horseracing was abolished, which led to the end of the park. Without the revenue from gambling, the park was unable to support the other attractions. The animals were sold off to Ringling Bros., private collectors and the city, which acquired a herd of elk, a Zebu cow, a bull and other animals. They were some of the first animals of the St. Louis Zoo. The only notable building in Fairground Park remaining from this bygone era is the Bear Pit.

Fairground Park was also the site of a large amphitheater, and when it was torn down, St. Louis built the city's first municipal swimming pool, in 1912. It was the largest municipal swimming pool in the country (some say in the world). It served up to ten thousand swimmers a day—white swimmers.

The pool became the location of a notorious race riot on June 21, 1949, after newly elected mayor Joseph Darst desegregated the swimming pool. This was the largest area race incident since the East St. Louis riots in 1917

Racial tension begins at Fairground Park swimming pool, June 21, 1949. *St. Louis Mercantile Library*.

(see chapter "Race Riots of East St. Louis, 1917"). The pool riot occurred after World War II, and there was a significant movement to make substantial social reforms. Why were Black men fighting Nazis (who believed that their race was inherently superior to all others), only to return to the United States and be refused the right to swim in a public pool?

The morning of June 21, thirty Black children and two hundred white children entered without incident. But soon, a group of unruly white people started to form outside the fence, many wielding sticks and clubs and shouting threats and racial slurs at the Black children. To avert possible violence, the police were called to escort the Black children from the park.

That evening, a group of about twenty to thirty Black youth was surrounded by white youth. The group of a few hundred whites grew to thousands (one account says five thousand), and 150 police officers responded in an effort to diffuse the situation. Order was for the most part restored by 10:00 p.m. Miraculously, there were no deaths during the riot; ten Black people and two white people were taken to the hospital. Only seven people were arrested, four Black and three white.

To avert a repeat of the dangerous situation, the mayor immediately reinstituted the segregation order. In 1950, the pool was again desegregated, this time without violence. Pool attendance, however, dropped by 80 percent, and by 1954, the city had to close the pool because revenues could no longer support its upkeep.

3715 NATURAL BRIDGE AVENUE, ST. LOUIS, MISSOURI 63107

THE FARMERS MARKET OLDER THAN
THE U.S. CONSTITUTION

*F*inding its way into the hearts of many St. Louisans, the Soulard Farmers Market sprang up in a field where local farmers sold their crops in 1779. The area is known as the Soulard District, named after a French surveyor named Antoine Soulard. He died in 1825, and in 1838, his widow, Julia, gifted two blocks of her property to the City of St. Louis with the stipulation that it be used as a public market in perpetuity.

In the early European colonial period, France claimed the area (naming it La Louisiane in honor of the French king Louis XIV in 1682). In 1762, Spain acquired the area west of the Mississippi after the Treaty of Fontainebleau. That meant little to the French, and in 1763, the French governor granted a trade monopoly over the west upper Mississippi region to Gilbert Antoine de St. Maxent, a French merchant from New Orleans. That said, the Spanish took possession of the trading post in the late 1760s; at least nominally, the region was under Spanish rule.

All the while, as France and Spain quibbled about functional ownership of the area, the British colonies on the eastern side of the continent were in the process of rebelling against the Crown. On July 4, 1776, the British rebels signed the Declaration of Independence. The ensuing war lasted until 1783. Four years later, leaders of the newly independent nation signed the Constitution of the United States on September 17, 1787.

Those who shopped at this marketplace lived under both French and Spanish rule fully eight years before the U.S. Constitution was signed. And

Soulard Market, 1910. *Missouri Historical Society.*

sixteen years later, they would find themselves under American law, following the Louisiana Purchase in in 1803.

The backstory to this vignette is that, as noted above, Antoine Soulard died in 1825, and his widow, Julia, inherited his estate. In 1836, the deed to his landholdings was questioned, and a five-year court battle ensued, after which the courts ruled in her favor. That is quite a battle, you say. But that is not the story. The story is that this took place in a French colony, governed by French law, and as such, Marie Julia Cérre Soulard could hold property and transact business.

Under *American* law (modeled after the English) of "coverture," a woman did not have a separate legal existence from her husband. A married English/American woman was considered a dependent of her husband (essentially the same status as a minor child) and could not own property or manage his business. If a couple had minor children, the wife could not even serve as their guardian. Had St. Louis been a British colony rather than a French one, it is likely Antoine Soulard's property would have been held in trust, and his wife would not have had control over it. These laws and customs only passed out of use during the middle of the nineteenth century.

The foundation of the current market was established in 1843, and in 1928, an entirely new and larger market was constructed on the site, which still stands today. One of the tenants, Schweiger's Produce, has been operated here since 1884 by the same family for four generations.

1713A SOUTH EIGHTH STREET, ST. LOUIS, MISSOURI 63104

FIRST BLACK CHURCH
IN ST. LOUIS

*T*he First Baptist Church on Bell Avenue opened its doors in 1818, three years before Missouri was admitted into the Union in 1821 and forty-seven years before the end of the Civil War in 1865. This means that for nearly half a century, this church served enslaved people who attended only with the permission of their owners.

By the mid-1840s, the church had a congregation of over five hundred. In this church, as in all Black churches of the time, slave owners used selected passages from the Bible, including 1 Peter 2:18 and Ephesians 6:5, where slaves are told to submit to their masters. All references to escaping from slavery (such as the exodus of the Hebrews from Egyptian captivity) were omitted.

Some of the nation's most ardent and irrefutable arguments for slavery, in fact, came from the Bible. The Old Testament has scores of references to slavery (even the Hebrews, God's chosen people, enslaved other tribes), and in the New Testament, Jesus lived during the occupation of Palestine by Rome, when slavery was a mainstay of the Roman economy—and he never mentions it as a moral injustice.

On the contrary, Christian southerners pointed to these biblical accounts to justify the enslavement of African Americans. A prominent theme revolved around the "curse of Ham," about Noah's second son. According to the account, Noah got drunk, and Ham "saw the nakedness of his father." For this, Noah cursed him, saying that Ham shall be the servant to his brethren. This was interpreted that Africans were descendants of

First Baptist Church, the first Black church in St. Louis, 1915. *Missouri Historical Society*.

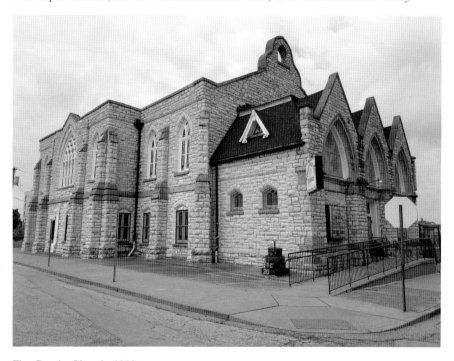

First Baptist Church, 2020.

Ham, and that God Almighty Himself ordained them to live in slavery because of this transgression.

Within the walls of Black churches, marriages were purely ceremonial. Since slaves were legally property, they could not enter into legally binding contracts. Married or not, with or without children, one member of a Black couple could be sold at will. As such, traditional Black wedding vows were, "Do you take this woman/man to be your spouse—until death or distance do you part?" At the end of the ceremony, it was common for couples to jump over a broom.

It wasn't until the end of the Civil War and the passage of the Thirteenth Amendment that slavery was abolished and emancipated Blacks gained the right to marry legally.

3100 BELL AVENUE, ST. LOUIS, MISSOURI 63106

FIRST COCKTAIL PARTY IN THE WORLD AND THE LARGEST COLLECTION OF MOSAICS

*I*n May 1917 at around noon, after church services let out, the world's first cocktail party was held in the parking lot of the Cathedral Basilica on Lindell Boulevard. About fifty people came to the party for drinks for about an hour, then lunch was served. The list of beverages included Scotch, bourbon, martinis, gin fizzes, Manhattans and Bronx cocktails.

The party was such a hit that it sparked interest in others in St. Louis and eventually nationwide. These public events were relatively short-lived, as Prohibition was introduced in December 1933.

There are a few versions of the exact location, with some stories citing the (now) parking lot of the basilica as the site, while other accounts say it was the location that later became the home of Archbishop John J. Glennon (purchased by the Catholic Church in 1924). Not that it really matters.

The church was consecrated in 1926 and replaced the Old Cathedral (on the banks of the Mississippi). In 1997, Pope John Paul II designated it as the Cathedral Basilica, and two years later, he visited St. Louis, and the Catholic community was enraptured by the visit. The church is renowned for its mosaics, which were installed from 1912 to 1988. There are over forty-one million individual pieces of glass in more than seven thousand colors covering 83,000 square feet, making it the largest collection of mosaics outside of Russia.

The back parking lot of the Cathedral Basilica, reputed to be the site of the first organized cocktail party in recorded history, in 1917. Photo taken of the area, 2020.

While this massive collection of mosaics is by no means an obscure fact about St. Louis, what is relatively unknown is that the basement of the cathedral contains a museum of the mosaics, their origin and construction.

4431 LINDELL BOULEVARD, ST. LOUIS, MISSOURI 63108

FIRST DRIVE-UP WINDOW

Top: Drive-through window at the Grand National Bank, 1930. *Missouri Historical Society*.

Bottom: The bricked-up window in 2020.

*A*s automobiles became more affordable, to the point where middle-class people could buy one, a local banker got the brainstorm to offer people banking services from the convenience of their cars.

In 1930, the modern twenty-two-story art deco Continental Life Building at Olive Street and North Grand Boulevard (on the same block as the Fox Theater) was home to the Grand National Bank. Since it was on the main floor, it proved ideal to accommodate a hole made in the wall in the alleyway and the installation of a teller's window.

The bank is no longer there. In 2000, the building was renovated into apartments. But if you are so inclined, you can drive through the alley to see the bricked-up window.

Continental Life Building, 3615 Olive Street, St. Louis, Missouri 63108

FIRST OLYMPICS IN THE USA

St. Louis was the location of the first Olympics held outside of Europe. The date: August 28, 1904. The place: Washington University's Francis Field and Gymnasium at Forsythe and North Big Bend Boulevards. The event was concurrent with the 1904 World's Fair, held in nearby Forest Park.

At this time, global tensions were high as the world watched the Russo-Japanese War, and this tension was reflected in the low participation at the games. Only twelve (or fifteen, depending on the source) nations were represented. There were 651 participants, of whom only 62 came from outside of North America. Equally interesting, there were only six female athletes.

One of the more curious sports was tug-of-war. It was an Olympic sport from 1900 to 1920. The Americans put on demonstrations of American football and basketball. During "Anthropology Days," there was an exhibit of archery conducted by African archers.

Boxing—men's and women's—debuted as a demonstration/exhibition sport at these Olympics. A total of eighteen boxers competed. The Olympic committee later decided to accept men's boxing but believed women's boxing posed a potential health risk, so it was not added to the official list of sports.

The Olympics featured the traditional marathon, but the conditions were deplorable. Temperatures in the nineties, terrible dust, a hilly trail and exhaust from automobiles made it so brutal that only twelve of the thirty-

The tug-of-war was an Olympic event in 1904! Here, the New York Athletic Club squares off against the Milwaukee Athletic Club. *Missouri Historical Society*.

Runners at Francis Olympic Field during the 1904 Olympics. *St. Louis Mercantile Library*.

one entrants finished. After three hours and thirteen minutes, one of the runners, Fred Lorz from New York, came across the finish line. None other than the president's daughter, Alice Roosevelt, gave him a floral wreath. He later confessed that he was losing badly and that when he realized he was out of contention, he caught a ride back (about a third of the overall distance) to the stadium to pick up his clothes. He said that he could not resist when the crowd started cheering.

The field has since been renamed the Francis Olympic Field, and both the field and gymnasium are in the National Register of Historic Places.

FORSYTH BOULEVARD AND NORTH BIG BEND BOULEVARD, ST. LOUIS, MISSOURI 63105

FOREST PARK'S AVIATION FIELD AND LINDBERGH'S AIRMAIL ROUTE

*I*t is a little-known fact that there used to be an airfield in the middle of Forest Park. After serving in the U.S. Army Air Service in 1924, barnstorming in the Midwest under the name "Daredevil Lindbergh" and working briefly as a mechanic in Billings, Montana, twenty-five-year-old Charles Lindbergh was an airmail pilot. He often flew the St. Louis–Chicago route. One account claims the idea of pursuing his transatlantic flight for the $25,000 Orteig Prize came to him while flying one of his long airmail routes.

Charles Lindbergh with "the first sack" of airmail to Chicago from Lambert Field. *National Archives Catalog.*

Among the several landing strips in St. Louis that he used, one is all but forgotten, replaced by four baseball and four softball fields that carry the nostalgic name Boeing Aviation Fields. There is nothing left of the airstrip except the name in the stone-and-concrete sign.

The average speed of aircraft flying airmail was about seventy-seven miles an hour, and the trip to Chicago was about three and a half hours.

FOREST PARK AVIATION FIELD, ST. LOUIS, MISSOURI 63110

FOREST PARK HIGHLANDS AND THE ST. LOUIS CAROUSEL

There are two "curvy" buildings south of Highway 40 next to St. Louis Community College, the Highland Plaza buildings. Why would an architect design them with such pronounced curves? It is because this is the former site of the Forest Park Highlands, a popular amusement park. It featured a giant rollercoaster called the Comet, and the two current buildings hearken back to the curve of the roller coaster. The building is also home to Comet Coffee, yet another reference to the roller coaster.

The park began in 1896 as the Highlands Cottage Restaurant, and within a year, a merry-go-round was built. By 1934, the site had evolved into the Forest Park Highlands Amusement Park, a popular attraction at 5600 Oakland Avenue, across from Forest Park. It operated for almost seven decades. At its zenith, it was a fourteen-acre park with fourteen major rides and nine kiddie rides. Sadly, it was dealt a fatal blow in 1963 when a massive fire destroyed most of it.

A block away (5700 Oakland Avenue) was the St. Louis Arena (later known as the Checkerdome), the country's second-largest indoor entertainment venue when it opened in 1929. It was located across I-64 opposite the Forest Park Aviation Field, where Charles Lindbergh used to land for his airmail route to Chicago (see chapter "Forest Park's Aviation Field and Lindbergh's Airmail Route").

One of the beloved rides, the St. Louis Carousel (built in 1929), was spared by the blaze. It featured sixty horses, four deer and two sleighs. With most of the other rides destroyed, the carousel was slated to be demolished.

The carousel was rescued from the burned-out remains of the amusement park and now operates (indoors) in Faust Park, 2020.

But a private citizen, Howard C. Ohlendorf, donated it to the St. Louis County Department of Parks and Recreation, which installed it in Sylvan Springs Park. It was later moved into an enclosed building in Faust Park in Chesterfield in 1987 to help preserve it from the elements.

In addition to the rides and concessions, Forest Park Highlands had the largest swimming pool in the Midwest and a dance hall. The entire park was a segregated, whites-only facility. Years ago, a Black professor friend of mine in his eighties related a story of visiting the park as a child and watching all the children on the rides. When he tried to enter, he was told that "colored people are not admitted."

FOREST PARK HIGHLANDS, 5600 OAKLAND AVENUE, ST. LOUIS, MISSOURI 63110

ST. LOUIS CAROUSEL, FAUST PARK, 15055 FAUST PARK, CHESTERFIELD, MISSOURI 63017

FROM BALLOON AGE
TO SPACE AGE

Few places in St. Louis emblemize the city's evolution as much as Lambert International Airport. It started off as the Kinloch Flying Field, a balloon-launching field established in 1909 by the St. Louis Aero Club, led by Albert Bond Lambert. In an era of lighter-than-air craft, it was the first club to have its own dedicated airfield.

Very early on, the site was the location of two historic events. On October 11, 1910, President Theodore Roosevelt boarded a Wright Type AB airplane with pilot Arch Hoxsey and became the first U.S. president to fly. An account states that Roosevelt "traveled twice around the aviation field in three minutes and twenty seconds. He waved his hands at the crowd of thousands on the field below." The event was captured on video, and you can view it online.

Two years later, in 1912, an aircraft took off from here and flew over Jefferson Barracks, where U.S. Army captain Albert Berry made the first parachute drop from an airplane. (Previous drops had been made from balloons.)

In 1913, the hangars were moved to a new location on North Broadway. In 1920, Kinloch Field was purchased by Major Albert Lambert. He had trained with Orville Wright and was the first St. Louisan to obtain a pilot's license. He moved the field to another site a few miles west, where he leased 170 acres and established the St. Louis Flying Field. In 1923, he renamed the field after himself, Lambert St. Louis Flying Field. Over the years, it evolved into today's St. Louis Lambert International Airport.

Above: President Theodore Roosevelt boarded a Wright Type AB airplane with pilot Arch Hoxsey, 1910. *Missouri Historical Society*.

Opposite: Captain Albert Berry (*standing*) with pilot Tony Jannus on March 1, 1912. Berry jumped from this Benoist-built biplane to become the first person to parachute from an airplane. *Missouri Historical Society*.

It was from this field that Charles Lindbergh left on May 12, 1927, for New York. From there, he began his famous nonstop solo flight to Paris. Lindbergh was familiar with St. Louis; in 1926, he became the chief pilot for Ryan Air, which flew airmail between Chicago and St. Louis (see chapter "Forest Park's Aviation Field and Lindbergh's Airmail Route"). Ryan Air moved to Lambert Field in 1928.

During World War II, Lambert was the home of several major aircraft manufacturers. Curtiss-Wright built the P-40 fighter, McDonnell Aircraft Company built the C-47 cargo aircraft and Robertson Aircraft Corporation built the WACO CG4 glider. In a sad tale, in 1943, Lambert Field was the scene of an accident involving the first "all–St. Louis built" WACO CG glider. It was carrying ten people, including Mayor William Becker, when the glider crashed before a crowd of ten thousand horrified spectators.

After the war, due to its central location, Lambert Field grew to become one of the biggest centers for commercial airlines. In the 1980s, it became one of the most important airports in the country and a hub for Trans World Airlines, which operated seventy gates here.

Lambert Field brought the nation into the space age. The nation's first astronauts went to space in capsules built by McDonnell Aircraft at Lambert.

McDonnell Aircraft Corporation engineers building the Mercury spacecraft in St. Louis, 1963. *NASA.*

A total of twenty Mercury spacecraft were delivered to NASA, six of which carried astronauts into space between 1961 and 1963. The country's first manned spaceflight was undertaken by astronaut Alan Shepard on May 5, 1961, aboard the *Freedom 7.* The following year, John Glenn piloted *Friendship 7* in the first U.S. human orbital flight, on February 20, 1962. The St. Louis Science Center has both a Mercury and a Gemini capsule on display (neither have been launched into space).

St. Louis Lambert International Airport, 10701 Lambert International Boulevard, St. Louis, Missouri 63145

FROM HORSES TO STREETCARS

*T*he success of a city depends largely on its ability to move people and goods. The small trading post on the west side of the Mississippi River was a conduit for trade of furs on and across the river, and as the city grew, the railroads and bridges (and later the roads, highways and airports) continued making St. Louis an ideal location for movement.

In those early days of industrialization, the city suffered from massive sprawl, as buildings and roads were thrown up out of expediency rather than planning, and infrastructure bringing in fresh water and dealing with sewage were secondary at best in the planning of the city. There was a great need to find increasingly more efficient ways to move goods. Initially, horses and wagons and carriages were the only viable options, but they left the city a stagnant dung heap and urinal for beasts of burden, with flies forming thick, black clouds in the famous summer heat. (Incidentally, you can find the last horse trough in St. Louis at the intersection of Ivory Avenue and Schimer Street in Carondelet.)

The first evolution in transportation came in 1838 with the introduction of the horse- or mule-drawn "horsecars." By the late 1850s, there was a complete horsecar railway system. You can see a mule car from the 1870s at the National Museum of Transportation.

Soon, another innovation arrived: the cable car. The year 1886 saw the first cable cars, wheeled coaches that latch on to underground cables. While they were an improvement over cars pulled by draft animals, the cables and pullies were prone to breaking and required continual maintenance and lubrication.

A mule car next to a streetcar on Jefferson Avenue, 1896. *Missouri Historical Society.*

Beginning in 1889, these began being replaced by electric streetcars, with overhead lines powering individual vehicles along rails. Within a decade, the cable-driven cars were gone. In October 1891, St. Louis began operating the first Railway Post Office under the direction of postmaster Major John B. Harlowe. In the 1920s, there was 485 miles of track in the St. Louis area with about 1,650 streetcars.

Streetcars dominated urban transportation for the next forty years, operating more than a dozen rail lines by dozens of companies. By the first part of the twentieth century, they had been unified into a single entity, the St. Louis Public Service Company. Lines ran over most major roads and across major bridges. At major junctures, businesses and residences grew to provide services to those using the lines.

Once automobiles appeared and grew in number, the surface road system began to increase, and in the 1920s, the streetcar system began to fade, replaced by buses for public transportation. The natural consequences of multiplying the number of vehicles began to catch up with the city, and pollution and road congestion became problematic. In 1939, St. Louis had the worst air pollution in the nation (see chapter "Choking on Progress:

The Worst Air Pollution in the Nation"), although this was primarily due to coal-burning factories and locomotives. Nonetheless, this was an era prior to unleaded gas and the catalytic converter, so vehicles were spewing out plenty of their own toxic gases. It was not until the early 1970s that unleaded gas was produced to reduce emissions, and not until 1975 were catalytic converters mandatory on U.S. automobiles. To ease congestion and to provide affordable transportation for those without private automobiles and to supplement the bus system, the city built a light-rail system in 1993, Metrolink, and St. Louis returned to the rails.

FUR, HIDES AND THE
EXTERMINATION OF THE BUFFALO

S t. Louis has been a center of the fur trade from its very inception. In 1838, Pierre Chouteau Jr. of the rich St. Louis Chouteau family bought the fur-trading rights in the Missouri River area from the Astor Fur Company, which was founded by John Jacob Astor, the United States' first millionaire. Astor traded with China for tea, sandalwood and other goods, including illegal Turkish opium (see chapter "Chinatown: Hop Alley and a President's Grandfather").

Initially, Chouteau was heavily involved in beaver pelts, but about 1850 that industry waned due to market saturation coupled with vast overhunting of beaver, so he began trading buffalo hides. Hunters delivered hides to Choteau at Fort Laramie, Wyoming, and Fort Pierre, South Dakota.

In the 1840s, Chouteau was receiving about 100,000 hides annually. Between 1843 and 1846, the shipments of buffalo hide through St. Louis doubled, contributing to the city's economic boom. By 1871, a single firm in St. Louis traded 250,000 hides.

Furs continued to be a critical component of St. Louis. In 1920, the International Fur Exchange opened on Fourth and Market Streets. At its peak, the Exchange building was where 80 percent of the world's seal, fox and beaver pelts were auctioned. Auction operations closed in 1950, and the Exchange building became part of the Drury Hotel.

The harvest of the buffalo for hides started reasonably enough. Like American beaver pelts, bison hides came into great demand as an exotic material. And hunting was part of westward expansion and Manifest

Left: The International Fur Exchange Building, 2020.

Below: The demand for buffalo hides was so high that hunters couldn't keep up. Rather than piecemeal hunting, they conducted industrial killing, hunting from trains. They could kill, skin and transport them with much greater efficiency. *Library of Congress*.

Destiny, glorifying how tough frontiersmen braved the wilderness to reap the natural bounty of the great fruited plains. There are a lot of omissions in that history.

The reality is that the buffalo population once totaled about twenty-five million, but by the late 1800s, there were less than four hundred wild buffalo in the United States. To meet the demand for hides, bands of hunters rode out to huge fields of buffalo to conduct industrial-scale hunting, shooting entire herds of thousands. They shot nonstop and had to use multiple rifles and even urinated on their overheated barrels to cool them so they could continue shooting. Hunters began a process of "hunting by rail," in which trains with hundreds of hunters pulled up to herds and shot from the windows or roofs, leaving thousands of dead buffalo.

At the end of the day, hunters would skin the animals, load their hides on the train and leave the carcasses to rot in the fields. In the winter, slicing open the chest cavity would produce clouds of warm steam in the cold air, and in the summer, the mounds of entrails would draw massive swarms of flies. Many buffalo were not killed outright but laid on the plains gasping and waiting to die among the legions of carcasses.

Beyond the monetary consideration, there were other, more Machiavellian motivations for hunting buffalo. The U.S. Army's objective in the West was to promote expansion, and the Native Americans were not particularly keen on the idea given their previous dealings with the government. The army was woefully undersized to cover the enormity of the frontier. To contend with this, the generals decided to control the indigenous people by eliminating one of their primary food sources. The technique was proven during the 1863–64 campaign against the Navajos, during which Colonel Kit Carson, an iconic frontier hero, destroyed tens of thousands of Navajo sheep to crush the tribe. This became the de facto U.S. policy. In 1872, Secretary of the Interior Columbus Delano wrote: "The rapid disappearance of game from the former hunting-grounds must operate largely in favor of our efforts to confine the Indians to smaller areas and compel them to abandon their nomadic customs."

INTERNATIONAL FUR EXCHANGE (NOW DRURY HOTEL), FOURTH AND MARKET STREETS, ST. LOUIS, MISSOURI 63102

THE GARMENT DISTRICT

Washington Avenue Second Only to New York

St. Louis' Garment District, located on Washington Avenue, was second only to New York City as a fashion center. Fashion was said to be equal in importance to beer and baseball. From the 1920s on, some of the most stylish women's clothing in the country was produced here. The city's designers began with beaver furs, then jeans and overalls, and of course shoes. The city was a leading producer of shoes, and Washington Avenue was dubbed "Shoe Street USA." St. Louis is often credited with introducing the concept of junior clothing. Previously, young women simply wore adult women's fashions in smaller sizes (although there is evidence that other areas of the country had done it earlier).

Long ago, all clothing was made at home by housewives. By the 1860s, all major cities had clothiers with tailors to produce ready-to-wear clothes. After a customer selected a suit, the tailor would hem the trousers or take in the waist. By the 1880s, the demand for cheap clothing led to factory assembly of clothing and of "sweating," the farming out of piecemeal work by individual "unskilled" workers. Almost all of these workers were women, most were immigrants and some were children—all of them worked long hours for low wages. Sweating is the source of the word *sweatshop*. We have iconic mental images of rooms crowded with dozens of women hunched over sewing machines, laboring in poorly lit rooms next to mounds of waiting fabric for twelve hours a day—for pennies.

The influx of immigrants left workers competing for jobs, any jobs, instituting a quasi-feudal system in which a freeman becomes a "wage slave." Workers were not paid by the hour but by the piece. If they did not produce,

Manufacturing shoes for the government, Brown Shoe Company, St. Louis, February 28, 1919. *U.S. National Archives and Records Administration.*

they did not get paid. As such, they worked feverishly for long hours. These conditions persisted until collectivization.

From 1934 to 1939, the clothing industry in St. Louis boomed. The number of women's clothing manufacturers tripled, and the number of garment workers went from 1,200 to 6,000. Annual sales went from $20 million to $85 million. St. Louis became the leading junior clothing manufacturer in the country.

Then World War II broke out, disrupting normal operations as production and raw materials were switched to uniforms, tents, canvas bags and army boots. When the war was over, production of regular clothing resumed. However, the increased cost of wages pushed manufacturers to find ways to reduce costs, including automation. More important, during the war, many businessmen made contacts in undeveloped countries. To reduce costs, they began shipping manufacturing jobs overseas to provide Americans with cheap clothing options. Major discount stores bought their goods and undercut domestic production, driving down pricing and slowly strangling domestic production.

GASLIGHT SQUARE

See Barbra Streisand for Two Bucks

*I*n 1961, for two dollars you could have purchased a ticket to see Barbra Streisand following the Smothers Brothers at the Crystal Palace in Gaslight Square.

From the early 1950s to the mid-'60s, the most happening place in town was found at Boyle and Olive Streets, home to fifty clubs, theaters, sidewalk cafés and antique shops. People flocked there to listen to jazz, enjoy a 1920s speakeasy with staged shootouts, enjoy drinks at a piano bar or listen to ragtime music in a club decked out like a riverboat.

The Musical Arts Building, on the southwest corner of Boyle and Olive, was a focal point. Local gal (and soon to be movie star) Betty Grable learned to dance there, opera star Helen Traubel studied voice there and a young Vincent Price's dentist had an office there. However, in 1959, a tornado swept through and damaged or destroyed many buildings.

But rather than destroying the area, the tornado brought insurance money to revitalize it. Businesses began to reopen, and everyone started calling the area Gaslight Square. In 1961, the board of aldermen renamed two blocks of Olive "Gaslight Square," and Laclede Gas later installed 121 gas streetlights to further instill the ambiance.

Many major entertainers of the era performed here early in their careers: Barbra Streisand, Jackie Mason, the Smothers Brothers, Lenny Bruce, Miles Davis, Mike Nichols and Elaine May, Woody Allen, Jerry Stiller, Dick Gregory and Jack E. Leonard. Allen Ginsberg even recited poetry to jazz. On April 17, 1961, the Smothers Brothers opened at the Crystal Palace, followed by eighteen-year-old Streisand.

A Dixieland band at Your Father's Moustache nightclub. *Missouri Historical Society*.

The streets around Boyle and Olive were swarmed by ten thousand people every night. The streets were so congested with foot traffic that it would take forty-five minutes to drive two blocks. But the party was short-lived. The crowds brought a certain degree of crime, including purse snatchers and car thieves. In 1964, a sixty-one-year-old artist named Lillian Heller was fatally shot during a robbery in her apartment in the neighborhood.

Crime, or the perception of crime, plus a change from a "Bohemian crowd" to a "mod hippy crowd," was concurrent with the district's demise. A few go-go bars appeared, and many factors started reducing the crowds— and the money. As quickly as it rose, Gaslight Square began to decay, and soon it was little more than a collection of vacant, dilapidated buildings.

By 1979, the entire area had been renovated with housing. The memory is marked by a monument with the names of the once-flourishing businesses and three faux Greek columns. The only business still in existence is O'Connell's Pub, which relocated to Shaw Boulevard south of I-44.

NORTH BOYLE AND OLIVE STREETS, ST. LOUIS, MISSOURI 63108

GERMAN SPY USES GERM WARFARE TO KILL MULES DURING WORLD WAR I

America's experience in World War I was dramatically different than in World War II. While the war raged from July 1914 to November 1918, the United States did not enter until December 1917. As such, the United States was involved in only the last thirteen months of the war. That said, America's entry into the war was a key factor in convincing the Central Powers (Germany, Austria-Hungary, Bulgaria and the Ottoman Empire) that defeat was inevitable.

Their one hope was to disrupt the flow of men and materiel across the Atlantic. To this end, their most famous effort was the employment of U-boats to sink supply ships. While this proved highly successful, it was not enough, and they sought other avenues to slow or stop war goods from getting to the front lines.

Another significant difference between the wars was one of mechanization. World War I made great use of railroads for transport, but there was little use of automobiles. A great deal of local transport of ammunition, weapons, food, medicine and other supplies was through beasts of burden. By war's end, the British army alone had 250,000 mules. They were an essential war commodity. Mules lived up to twice as long as horses, had great endurance and recovery, were surefooted and could eat forage like natural grasses found en route, instead of oats required for horses.

The problem in wartime is that draft animals die from any number of hazards (starvation, sickness, illness, wounds from artillery and other military causes or simply being worked to death), and they take a long time

A poisoned horse in World War I, credited to German agents. *National Archives.*

to replace. In 1914, the nation of Germany had four million horses and mules. England and France together could muster only six million, but America had a whopping twenty-five million. When America entered the fray, it was a godsend to the Triple Entente of Great Britain, France and Russia. This was especially notable when, in March 1918, Russia dropped out of the war.

American mules were shipped from the interior of the United States to, primarily, Newport News, Virginia, then sent by boat to England. Missouri was by far the largest exporter of mules during the war, and the Guyton and Harrington Mule Company was the largest. It had six thousand acres of pasture with eighteen buildings—the world's largest horse barns (dubbed "mule palaces"). They were a city block long and a half block wide. From 1914 to 1918, the company sold 180,000 mules to the British army, about half of all mules sent to Britain.

To transport the animals to the East Coast, suppliers were able to secure three railroads—the Santa Fe, the Rock Island and the Burlington lines—to connecting lines from their rural facilities. These connected to other lines, most of which ran through St. Louis and on to holding pens and shipyards in Virginia. During the war, 457,000 horses and mules passed through Newport News alone.

The Germans were intent on disrupting or destroying this vital pipeline. They instituted a plan to have German agents specializing in biochemistry infect the American mules and horses with anthrax and an equine disease called glanders. The United States would be forced to turn off the flow of mules to avoid the risk of infecting animals in Europe.

The key agent in this program was Dr. Anton Dilger, an American of German heritage, along with a small group of saboteurs. Dilger set up a lab in a two-story brick house on Thirty-Third Street in Washington, D.C., where he started a doctor's office (which saw no patients). During 1915–16, he and his team were successful in killing thousands of horses and mules in pens on the Eastern Seaboard.

Operations ceased in July 1916 after what became known as the Black Tom explosion in New Jersey, which destroyed a munitions factory that supplied ammunition to the Allies. Dilger's good friend Fred Herrmann moved the lab to St. Louis in September—without Dilger. The saboteurs noted that St. Louis was a concentrated shipping point and that the city had a significant number of Germans, but they discovered that few were willing to take the risk of helping them. Herrmann ran the new lab, but since he lacked Dilger's medical knowledge, he was unable to grow the bacteria, and the operation ended.

Federal investigators interviewed Dilger several times, but he was not arrested, and as things heated up, he left for Mexico. He later received the German Iron Cross for service to his homeland.

THE GIRL IN THE SHADOW BOX

A Tale of Unrequited Love

O ne of the most alluring and beautiful monuments in historical Bellefontaine Cemetery is the "Girl in the Shadow Box," the tomb of Herman Luyties, by Italian sculptor Giulio Monteverde, carved in 1921. This sculpture and its backstory transcend its purpose as a memorial. The monument stands as a watchful sentinel in perpetuity over Herman Luyties, a St. Louisan who made his fortune in pharmaceuticals.

While traveling to Italy in the 1900s, Luyties met and fell hard for a voluptuous model. He proposed to her and she declined, which left him brokenhearted. In an effort to retain a small piece of her, he commissioned famed sculptor Giulio Monteverde to create a twelve-foot-tall marble statue of his love as an angel.

For the commission, Monteverde created a duplicate of one of his earlier sculptures, *The Angel of Oneto*, a female winged angel that he carved for a wealthy Genoese merchant named Francisco Oneto. (It stands in Staglieno Cemetery.) The duplicate he created for Luyties differs in the hair and face, and it does not have wings.

Luyties shipped the sculpture to his home in St. Louis and had it installed in the foyer of his mansion. Its weight was apparently too much for the home, so he decided to move it to a burial plot in Bellefontaine Cemetery.

In the statue's new outdoor location, the St. Louis weather began to deteriorate the marble. To prevent further deterioration, Luyties built a stone case and had it enclosed in glass, protecting it without depriving the

"Girl in the Shadow Box," ever watchful over the tomb of Herman Luyties, carved in 1921 by Italian sculptor Giulio Monteverde, 2020.

world of its beauty. The memorial was thereafter known as the Girl in the Shadow Box. In 1921, at age fifty, Luyties died and was buried at its feet. He is forever watched over by his one, eternal love.

BELLEFONTAINE CEMETERY, 4947 WEST FLORISSANT AVENUE, ST. LOUIS, MISSOURI 63115

THE GREAT CYCLONE OF 1896

O n May 27, 1896, the third-deadliest tornado in the nation's history tore through St. Louis. It cut a swath three miles long through the city, killing between 255 and 306 people and injuring another 1,000. In its wake, it left the mangled wreckage of houses, factories and businesses. When it hit the Mississippi River, it sucked up entire steamboats and other vessels, crushed them and scattered the rubble across both banks of the river. The Eads Bridge (the first major bridge constructed by making use of steel and considered to be tornado-proof), only twenty-two years old at the time, lost approximately three hundred feet of its eastern approach.

The roof torn off a kiosk with uprooted trees. The statue of Senator Thomas Hart Benton (which still stands today) can be seen in the background. *Missouri Historical Society*.

Damage to Eads Bridge and shipwrecks following the Great Cyclone of 1896. *Missouri Historical Society.*

The tornado hit the edge of the Missouri Botanical Garden, but Lafayette Park, the oldest park west of the Mississippi, was directly in its path and was utterly destroyed. Horrific winds uprooted virtually every tree, hurling them blocks away, and demolished every structure but one. The iron fence ringing the park was twisted and torn beyond repair.

One thing that did survive was a bronze statue of Senator Thomas Hart Benton, built in 1868 by sculptor Harriet Hosmer (barely visible in the accompanying photo). It holds two distinctions: the first monument west of the Mississippi River, and the first public monument in America created by a woman.

So many of the homes of the city's elite neighborhood were destroyed or damaged that most of the wealthy moved to a new neighborhood, the Central West End.

2023 LAFAYETTE AVENUE, ST. LOUIS, MISSOURI 63104

THE GREAT FIRE OF 1849

*O*n May 17, 1849, a fire originating on a riverboat spread throughout the largely wood buildings of St. Louis, destroying a third of the city—a full fifteen blocks, 418 buildings and twenty-three steamboats. The financial loss amounted to between $2.5 and $6 million, depending on the source (in 1849 dollars). Miraculously, only a handful of deaths were reported.

Known as the "Great Fire," the blaze originated on the steamboat *White Cloud*, moored at the docks situated at the heart of the present-day Arch grounds. Men fought the flames, but the fire burned through the ropes, and soon the flaming vessel floated into other vessels and the wharf, igniting them along with huge stacks of cargo.

The fire spread rapidly through downtown and along Locust and Vine Streets, which were occupied by wooden shanties. A second fire consumed almost everything on nine blocks north of Market Street. It then turned toward the Old Cathedral at Walnut and Third Streets. It was only arrested after officials ordered six buildings be blown up at Market and Second Streets (now the Arch grounds) with kegs of black powder. The act spared the Old Cathedral from being incinerated.

However, the explosions killed at least three people, including Captain Thomas Targee of Missouri Company No. 5, who was killed spreading powder in the Phillips Music Store. Targee became a hero, and in 1893, the city renamed Johnson Street in his honor. Thirteen years later, in 1906, Josephine Baker was born. She lived in the urban slums of Targee Street.

Print of "Great Fire at St. Louis, Mo.," illustrating the explosion of the riverboat *White Cloud* on Thursday, May 17, 1849. *Missouri Historical Society*.

The slums were later demolished and became the site of the Municipal Auditorium (see chapter "Josephine Baker: The Opera House Built over Her Childhood Slum").

After the fire, with so much of the housing and businesses (and jobs) destroyed, thousands of people were homeless, jobless and destitute. This in turn fueled crime. In response, many residents moved to Chicago. During rebuilding, the city required significant fireproofing codes, including the use of brick. New structures that emerged were now four or five stories with heavy brick walls with stone or cast-iron façades.

As for the Old Cathedral, the present building is the fourth church to be erected on the site. Construction began in 1831, and it was dedicated in 1834. The firestorm added misery to the city's worst single disaster later that summer, a cholera epidemic that killed 10 percent of the population (see chapter "Cholera Outbreak of 1849 Kills 10 Percent of Population").

BASILICA OF SAINT LOUIS, KING OF FRANCE (OLD CATHEDRAL), 209 WALNUT STREET, ST. LOUIS, MISSOURI 63102

THE GREAT ST. LOUIS BANK ROBBERY

So You Want to Be in Pictures

*T*he Southwest Bank Building at Kingshighway and Southwest (recently turned into BMO Harris) is a well-known landmark. It stands at the base of The Hill, St. Louis' Italian neighborhood renowned for its dozens of fine restaurants and tidy houses.

The bank is also the site of the nation's largest bank heist, in 1953. The crime inspired the movie *The Great St. Louis Bank Robbery* with Steve McQueen. (Incidentally, many of the people in the movie were not actors; they were the people who were present during the actual robbery.)

The Southwest Bank building's exterior was preserved during a recent renovation, 2020.

On April 24, the bank was entered by three Chicago gangsters, including ringleader Fred W. Bowerman, a sixty-year-old veteran criminal on the FBI's Ten Most Wanted list. The group planned the heist in the corner of the beautiful Tower Grove Park just down the street. The robbers nabbed $140,000 and tried to escape, but police were nearby and, in a hail of gunfire, thwarted their effort.

Bowerman died a week after the incident, and the other two men were apprehended and given long sentences.

The signature golden eagle with wings outspread perched on the clock on top of the building today was not part of the original building. In 2018, as BMO Harris, the building underwent an extensive renovation.

BMO HARRIS BANK, 2301 SOUTH KINGSHIGHWAY BOULEVARD, ST. LOUIS, MISSOURI 63110

HOME AND CASTLE

O ne really cannot get an appreciation for St. Louis history without examining some of the city's most famous historical homes. For the most part, this book does not address topics or places that are extremely well known—Anheuser-Busch, the Cardinals, the Arch—because these are exhaustively dealt with elsewhere. The following homes are an exception to that rule, because they have been well preserved, and visiting them offers us a firsthand view of the past.

That said, it is important to understand what we are looking at. These historical homes are not representative of "regular" people's residences, with the possible exception of the Hanley House, which is an example of a larger, successful working farm.

To understand what these homes mean, they must be framed in the world of the early 1900s. In 1911, a blast furnace factory worker earned 37¢ an hour and worked seventy hours per week. The median family income was about $490 a year. Much of the population was immigrant, and many of those were Catholic with large families. About 20 percent of people lived in extremely crowded conditions, often with whole families sharing one or two rooms. Smaller children often shared beds and almost always shared rooms. Parents often shared beds with children, particularly when they were young. A new home in 1900 was about 700 to 1,200 square feet with two or three bedrooms and one bathroom. Occasionally, one or more homes would even share a bathroom.

CHATILLON-DeMENIL MANSION

This home originated in 1849 as a four-bedroom brick residence built by a guide and hunter for the American Fur Company, Henri Chatillon. In 1856, Chatillon sold the property to a wealthy Frenchman named Dr. Nicholas DeMenil, who married Emilie Sophie Chouteau, a descendent of the founder of the city. In 1861, DeMenil began expanding the home into a Greek Revival mansion. He died in 1882, leaving the home to his son, who died in 1928. In 1945, the caves beneath the property (Cherokee Cave) were turned into a tourist attraction. In the 1960s, I-55 was routed to run through the area, and the mansion was slated for demolition,

Chatillon-DeMenil Mansion.

but the Landmarks Association of St. Louis bought the property from the Missouri Highways and Transportation Commission with a gift from Union Electric. It is not the most lavish of homes; it has what Italians would call "grandezza sbiadita"—faded grandeur.

CHATILLON-DeMENIL MANSION, 3352 DeMENIL PLACE, ST. LOUIS, MISSOURI 63118

Clester Cabin.

CLESTER CABIN

Built in the late 1700s, the Clester Cabin in Creve Coeur is one of the oldest structures in St. Louis County. It is one of the few remaining settler cabins of St. Louis' early period, typical of frontier homes—a one-room structure with a fireplace and a loft. Most of a family's life was spent outside of the home, which was mainly safe shelter from the elements and hostilities, and its primary role was for sleeping and cooking. The cabin's name comes from the family that oversaw its restoration rather than its original builder or occupants. It was originally built on the other side of I-270 (where Mercy Hospital now stands) and was relocated to its current site in 1994.

CLESTER CABIN, CONWAY PARK, 12301 CONWAY ROAD, CREVE COEUR, MISSOURI 63141

HANLEY HOUSE

Hanley House.

Built in 1855, the Hanley House (home of the family that lends its name to Hanley Road) is the oldest structure in the City of Clayton. The house is an exemplary and well-maintained example of a larger working-class farmhouse of the period. Today, it serves as a museum of life in the late 1800s, with many of the original family furnishings and artifacts. It stands in stark contrast to opulent homes such as the Campbell House or Cupples House; it has none of the lavish trappings of the wealthy. Many of the artifacts and household features are considerably more utilitarian. The family was Confederate and owned slaves. Behind the home is a cooking area/dwelling for a slave, and slaves worked on the farm itself. The home offers an unvarnished, accurate view of life in a slave state during that era. The curator's narration is fascinating and helps one understand life for the inhabitants, as well as other issues such as child mortality, slavery and the labor that was necessary to survive.

HANLEY HOUSE, 7600 WESTMORELAND AVENUE, CLAYTON, MISSOURI 63105

ROBERT G. CAMPBELL HOUSE

Built in 1851, the Campbell House was the first home in the elegant Lucas Place neighborhood. An Irish immigrant, Robert Campbell was a fur trader and entrepreneur. After doing quite well in the fur trade, he turned to dry goods, banking, real estate and river trading. The house is designed in the Greek Revival style applied to a Victorian townhouse. It is the sole survivor of Lucas Place. In 1854, Campbell purchased the house and began furnishing it with furniture from Philadelphia and making modifications to the structure.

Robert G. Campbell House.

The museum today contains hundreds of the family's original possessions: extraordinary furniture, fixtures, paintings and personal possessions. The home is well maintained and underwent major restorations in 1999 and 2005.

ROBERT G. CAMPBELL HOUSE, 1508 LOCUST STREET, ST. LOUIS, MISSOURI 63103

SAMUEL CUPPLES HOUSE

Built in 1890, the Romanesque Revival Samuel Cupples House (on the Saint Louis University campus) is a monument to the period craftsmen from Scotland who carved the decorative stonework. The house was one of the largest and most impressive of its time; it has three floors and exceeds twenty-five thousand square feet. It houses gorgeous Tiffany stained

Samuel Cupples House.

glass, a round turret and period furnishings. A grand library, music hall, great halls, salons and sitting rooms are all as they were in their heyday. It boasts forty-two rooms and twenty-two fireplaces. The primary building material of the home is brick, but it also includes purple granite from Colorado and pink granite from Missouri. In 1900, a total of eighteen people inhabited the home, most of whom were servants. The cost for constructing the home today is estimated to be around $15 million.

SAMUEL CUPPLES HOUSE, 3673 WEST PINE BOULEVARD, ST. LOUIS, MISSOURI 63103

SLAVE CABIN

Slave cabin.

In stark contrast to even a typical low-income home of the 1900s, the slave cabin at the Griot Museum of Black History barely qualifies as human habitation. It is not a re-creation; like all of these other homes, this is the genuine article. It is one of sixteen slave cabins from the Wright Smith Tobacco Plantation near Jonesburg in Montgomery County, about sixty miles west of St. Louis. It is made of oak and chestnut logs with V-notched construction. It offers the most rudimentary of shelter from the elements and would have had a dirt floor and no plumbing. The furnishings would include only whatever basic items the occupants could make. Millions of people lived in places and conditions such as these.

GRIOT MUSEUM OF BLACK HISTORY, 2505 ST. LOUIS AVENUE, ST. LOUIS, MISSOURI 63106

HOOVERVILLE

Slums on the Arch Grounds

hat U.S. city had the largest shantytown during the Great Depression? Yes, St. Louis. The population of people living in clusters of dilapidated makeshift shelters reached a peak of about five thousand—roughly the size of present-day Fenton or Glendale.

During the Depression, St. Louis was the seventh-largest city in the nation, and unemployment peaked at 30 percent in 1933 – far above the national average. Without income, whole families (mainly in the middle class) lost homes and had to move in with family or friends. Those with no other options built hovels or shanties made of discarded lumber, crates or other people's junk.

Across the country, these shanties clustered into little shantytowns, and collectively they were named after the person the inhabitants identified as the cause: President Herbert Hoover. This was the birth of the term *Hooverville*. These nonpermanent communities were without running water, toilets, adequate housing, food, clothing, police protection or jobs.

In an effort to maintain a level of normalcy during very abnormal circumstances, residents of St. Louis' Hooverville held school, built their own church out of orange crates and had an unofficial mayor. The city's Hooverville formed around the area where people were already living "off the grid"—on houseboats on the Mississippi River riverfront south of MacArthur Bridge. The land was owned by Terminal Railroad, which rented spots to squatters for one dollar a month.

St. Louis' Hooverville stretched for more than a mile along the riverfront, just south of the Municipal (present-day MacArthur) Bridge, circa 1930. *Missouri History Society.*

Residents lived by performing piecemeal labor and salvaging. One can imagine people took to any number of less savory enterprises to make money. Almost all were reliant, to some degree, on charities, churches and local merchants. Grocers at Soulard Market sent unsold food, and other city residents formed a charity called the Welcome Inn that served up to four thousand meals a day.

As time passed, the economy gradually improved, and St. Louis' Hooverville began to shrink. The remnant bits and pieces were eventually deemed a public eyesore, and in the 1950s, it was bulldozed. For seven years, the empty space on the riverfront was turned into a carnival, with roller coasters and exhibits. Seven years later, construction began on the Gateway Arch Grounds.

GATEWAY ARCH NATIONAL PARK, 11 NORTH FOURTH STREET, ST. LOUIS, MISSOURI 63102

HOW PIGGLY WIGGLY
SHAPED SHOPPING

The major economic and technological changes in our world often dwarf those that affect us the most. Take household shopping. People used to shop for food in a very different fashion, and we've all but forgotten it today.

First, stores were specialized. That is, they only carried one type of food—butcher, green grocer, fishmonger, dairy or dry goods (boxed or canned goods) store.

Stores were small. It would be pointless to stock more food than could reasonably be sold (in a day or two for meat and dairy, a little longer for fruit and vegetables). And women (and only women shopped) had to either walk or take a streetcar, depending on the era. It was troublesome carrying a lot of groceries, and in the summer, the heat was a problem for perishables. And most women had to bring children, either to help carry smaller parcels or because they had no one at home to watch them.

These factors meant that small stores were in every neighborhood. It also meant that a woman's shopping consisted of frequent smaller trips to several stores every day or two.

Another major difference from today is that shoppers would walk to a counter and present the clerk with a list, and the clerk (always a man) then retrieved the goods himself, picking the fruits, meats and so on. If you liked your carrots larger or your peaches ripe, you indicated your preference. The clerk would pick, weigh, bundle and bag your purchases and calculate the tab.

With the coming of industrialization, packaging started becoming standardized. Earlier, your bag of walnuts was scooped out of bins, like bulk foods today, into a small bag. With the introduction of packaged goods, your

Interior of a Piggly Wiggly self-service grocer in Memphis, 1918. *Library of Congress.*

oatmeal now came in a uniform box. And this of course meant consistent sizes of packing and ease of pricing (rather than having the clerk weigh everything).

One of the biggest changes came in 1920, when the Piggly Wiggly market opened. To reduce labor costs, they eliminated the grocery clerk and put the goods on shelves. Customers would walk around and pick up items they wanted. Since dry goods in particular were now standardized, clerks were no longer needed to calculate prices and bundle food, and the position was replaced by a cashier.

The new model drove the price of food so low that other stores had to adopt the model or go out of business. So they did. Other companies began forming stores carrying multiple foods (meats, dairy, greens) and put the goods out for customers to serve themselves.

The Piggly Wiggly model exploded. The owners capitalized on their success after inventing the concept of franchising independent self-serve grocers. Piggly Wiggly introduced the model in Memphis in 1916, and within one year, there were 9 in town. By 1923, there were nearly 1,300 of them in Tennessee. The company's plan was to establish 1 store for every ten thousand people in every city of any size in the United States.

Meat counter at a St. Louis grocery store, 1928. *Missouri Historical Society.*

St. Louis had more than thirty-five stores at one point, Chicago had fifty, Memphis had fifteen or twenty and there were plans to open thirty-five in Oakland. Soon they were everywhere. There was no going back, and every new grocer had to adopt similar models to contain costs and optimize efficiency in order to survive.

Believe it or not, you can look up old Piggly Wiggly (and other) grocer locations on a website titled Groceteria.com, with a section titled "St. Louis Chain Grocery/Supermarket Locations, 1933–1975": www.groceteria. com/place/us-missouri/st-louis/.

Here are some places that used to be a Piggly Wiggly:

BLUEPRINT COFFEE, 6225 DELMAR BOULEVARD, ST. LOUIS, MISSOURI 63130

INSOMNIA COOKIES, 226 NORTH EUCLID AVENUE, ST. LOUIS, MISSOURI 63108

TREE HOUSE RESTAURANT, 3177 SOUTH GRAND BOULEVARD, ST. LOUIS, MISSOURI 63118

BRASSERIE BY NICHE, 4580 LACLEDE AVENUE, ST. LOUIS, MISSOURI 63108

JOSEPHINE BAKER

The Opera House Built over Her Childhood Slum

*T*here is much written about world-famous Josephine Baker's life after leaving St. Louis in 1920: world-class singer, spy and activist. Here are two amazing revelations about her life while she was in St. Louis.

Revelation number one is that she was born on June 3, 1906, at the Female Hospital of Saint Louis, located in what is now Sublette Park on The Hill. Thirty-one years earlier, the hospital had been renamed from the Social Evil Hospital. This was the hospital established for prostitutes and unwed mothers after St. Louis became the first city in the United States to legalize prostitution (see chapter "Social Evil Hospital: First U.S. City to Legalize Prostitution").

Born to two impoverished mixed-race parents, Josephine lived at 212 Targee Street near Union Station, between Market Street and Clark Avenue. The street was renamed for the fireman who died in the Great Fire of 1849 (see chapter "The Great Fire of 1849"). It was a racially mixed area of low-income apartments, boardinghouses and brothels without indoor plumbing.

When her brother Richard was born, Josephine's father abandoned the family. Her mother could barely provide for them, and Josephine was raised hungry and poor, playing in the rail yards of Union Station.

When Josephine was eight years old, her mother put her to work as a servant girl in the home of a white woman. She had to sleep in the coal cellar with the dog and was punished for using too much soap in the laundry by having her hands scalded.

The Kiel Auditorium (formerly Municipal Auditorium), 2020.

At times, Josephine lived as a street child in the slums, sleeping in cardboard shelters and scavenging food from people's trash. At age thirteen, she worked as a waitress at the Old Chauffeur's Club at 3133 Pine Street. She married by age fourteen and divorced by age fifteen.

The massive race riots in East St. Louis took place in 1917, and she left St. Louis three years later. In 1925, between the First and Second World Wars, Josephine moved to France. In 1927, she was the first Black person to star in a major motion picture, the silent film *Siren of the Tropics*. She rose to international fame on the stage in Europe, where she became known as "La Baker" in her adopted France.

She returned to St. Louis several times after World War II to see her mother, but she was always resentful of the racial discrimination that still existed, and she refused to play to segregated audiences. In 1951, she was invited to perform at the Chase Hotel for $12,000 but refused because Blacks were not permitted to attend.

On February 3, 1952, she agreed to perform in St. Louis for the first time since becoming famous. At the end of the performance, she gave a long speech against racial discrimination. The venue was the Kiel Auditorium (originally known as the Municipal Auditorium).

And this brings us full circle to revelation number two: the Municipal Auditorium was built in 1933 over Targee Street, the street of Josephine's childhood home. Yes, she performed in St. Louis' premiere opera house, which was built on top of the very street where she had foraged for scraps of food in alleys of the slums.

212 TARGEE STREET, ST. LOUIS, MISSOURI
KIEL AUDITORIUM, 1401 CLARK AVENUE, ST. LOUIS, MISSOURI 63103

LAVISH DINNER PARTY INSIDE THE MILL CREEK SEWER

*I*n the earliest days of St. Louis, there was no concept of sewers as we know them today. People simply dumped their waste in the dirt roads or into the rivers. As late as 1969, the year we put a man on the moon, St. Louis dumped 95 percent of its sewage into the Mississippi untreated.

From the earliest years, two of St. Louis' rivers, River Des Peres and Mill Creek, became de facto open sewers. In 1766, one of them, Mill Creek, was dammed up, which in three years created a large lake in the middle of St. Louis that became known as Chouteau's Pond.

Over decades, the accumulated sewage led to numerous outbreaks of cholera, culminating in a massive outbreak in 1849 that killed 10 percent of the population (see chapter "Cholera Outbreak of 1849 Kills 10 Percent of Population"). Following that, city health officials drained the lake.

Prior to the 1904 World's Fair, city officials selected Forest Park for the site of the exposition, and the River Des Peres ran right through it. Determined not to let the foul river ruin the fair, planners built a wooden structure over it and covered it with earth. The structure worked fine for several years, but in 1915, there was exceptionally heavy rainfall, resulting in massive flooding that overpowered the sewers.

The city decided to create permanent sewers with sufficient capacity to handle all potential flow. In 1916, the Mill Creek Sewer was completed. To celebrate, the city and Mayor H.W. Kiel held a lavish party within the (as yet unused) sewers, charging twenty-five-dollars a plate.

In 1923, the city started plans for the River Des Peres, which would become the largest sewer system of its kind, a thirteen-mile network of sewers and drainage channels. Construction ran from 1924 to 1931. The project was named The River Des Peres Sewage & Drainage Works and called for the creation of a pair of side-by-side, twenty-nine-foot-diameter concrete tunnels, one each for sewage and stormwater.

This was just a transport system, and the plan was to continue dumping untreated sewage into rivers that emptied into the Mississippi. It was considered one of the engineering marvels of its day. There is an entrance to the tunnels in Forest Park.

You can see another place where the river disappears and enters the sewer, behind the intersection of Harvard and Dartmouth Avenues in University City. You cannot see it from the public streets, but it is visible on Google Maps.

You cannot see any aboveground features for some distance. The underground river flows down Lindell to Union, through the park and beneath Bowl Lake and Jefferson Lake in the southeast part of the park. You can see the plaque dedicated to the sewer project. The river continues south under I-64 and flows under the St. Louis Science Center and Saint Louis University High School.

You finally get an unobstructed view of two massive tunnels while looking east from the bridge on Macklind (south of Manchester) that crosses the River Des Peres. (It is not really a river, but a concrete culvert.) Immediately

Opposite: Mayor H.W. Kiel held a lavish party in the Mill Creek sewer when it was completed, 1916. *Missouri Historical Society*.

Above: Chouteau's Mill Creek, east from Thirteenth and Gratiot, showing construction of Mill Creek Sewer, 1868. *Missouri Historical Society*.

south of the bridge is a service road that leads east toward the huge openings. It terminates at a chain-link fence, but you can get close enough to see.

The Metropolitan Sewer District was not formed until 1954, and its first wastewater treatment facility, Coldwater Creek in Florissant, did not open until 1965. As late as 1969, only 5 percent of St. Louis' sewage was treated before being released into the Mississippi. Today, approximately seven hundred older cities still dump untreated sewage into their waterways.

MASTERPIECE HIDDEN
IN U-HAUL'S CEILING

*T*his story begins, strangely, when four men started a firm called the American Stove Company in 1901. St. Louisans will recognize it by the name it began using in 1951: Magic Chef.

In 1946, soon after World War II was over, the booming company erected an office building at 1641 South Kingshighway, just north of I-44 today, and the plans included a modern art ceiling by noted sculptor Isamu Noguchi.

Noguchi designed the plaster-and-glass ceiling as one of his final large-scale *Lunar Landscape* sculptures. The other two were in a stairwell aboard the ocean liner SS *Argentina* and in the Time-Life Building in New York.

The reason Noguchi did not begin the project until 1946 is because he was at a Japanese internment camp. Some readers may be unfamiliar with the history, so we should clarify this World War II story. These camps were not Japanese-run camps to hold American POWs, nor were they American-run camps to hold Japanese POWs. These were camps operated by the U.S. War Relocation Authority, on American soil, to imprison U.S. citizens of Japanese ancestry.

Noguchi was born in Los Angeles to a Japanese father and a mother of European ancestry. The law, strangely, applied only to Japanese on the West Coast. He was from New York, so the law did not pertain to him. Nonetheless, he was able to get "self-interned" to try to work with government officials to improve the camps. He was admitted to the Poston camp in Arizona, becoming one of the 120,000 American citizens imprisoned during the war. After only two months, he was dismayed by the lack of progress, and he

Lunar Landscape by noted sculptor Isamu Noguchi in the ceiling of the U-Haul building on South Kingshighway, 2020.

sought to leave. Apparently, it was a lot easier to self-admit than self-depart, and he was not able to leave for another seven months. Eventually, he was successful and returned to New York.

But back to the ceiling. Due to economic changes, Magic Chef closed its St. Louis plants, and in 1958, the owners sold the company. The Teamsters Union occupied the building briefly, but then it sat vacant for at least ten years. In 1977, U-Haul purchased the building. As part of the renovation, the exterior was bricked up and the interior was remodeled, including the lobby. The magnificent modern art ceiling was covered in a drop ceiling. For some reason, in 2016, U-Haul removed the drop ceiling, revealing the work of art after ten years of concealment. You can walk in and see it today.

U-HAUL, 1641 SOUTH KINGSHIGHWAY BOULEVARD, ST. LOUIS, MISSOURI 63110

MIRACLE AUTHENTICATED BY THE VATICAN

The only miracle in the Midwest authenticated by the Vatican took place at St. Joseph's Church on Eleventh Street. The original church was built by Jesuits in 1843. It was home to a relic of Peter Claver, a Spanish Jesuit who was held to have great intercessory powers with God. He would board slave ships to provide care and comfort to terrified Africans. He was canonized in 1888. The plaque at this statue in St. Joseph's (visible in the accompanying photo) lists him as "Patron Saint of Negros."

About the miracle: in 1864, a German immigrant named Ignatius Strecker was injured working at a local soap factory.

The statue of St. Joseph at St. Joseph Church, 2020.

Medical care was ineffective, and Strecker grew worse until doctors told him he had two weeks to live. Shortly after, Strecker struggled to church, and the priest was blessing the congregation with a relic of Claver. The priest allowed Strecker to kiss the relic, and the story goes that Strecker started recovering almost immediately. Within days he was back at work, and months later was back to full health.

In 1866, the Catholic Church conducted a canonical investigation, and the Vatican declared the incident to be a miracle, resulting in the canonization of Peter Claver. In 1867, the church built an elaborate altar, known as "The Altar of Answered Prayers," a replica of St. Ignatius in the Jesuit Gesu Church in Rome.

SHRINE OF ST. JOSEPH, 1220 NORTH ELEVENTH STREET, ST. LOUIS, MISSOURI 63106

THE MISSISSIPPI

Giving Birth to Everything

he indigenous Anishinaabe called it Misi-ziibi ("Great River"). It
is the fourth-largest river in the world and today provides water to
over eighteen million people every day. The river provided for the
reliable and economical transportation of the fruit of the frontier to Europe
and the eastern part of the United States, inexorably dictating where we
would build our cities, roads and rails.

The French established settlements where they traded with local tribes,
and the Spanish had missions and their own outposts. Ultimately, the
fledgling United States purchased the Louisiana Territory (which included
St. Louis) from the French in 1803, effectively doubling the landmass of the
nation. At this time, St. Louis was but one of many small French trading
outposts, having been established in 1764, roughly forty years earlier.

Famously, Jefferson appointed Meriwether Lewis and William Clark to
explore the new territory with an expedition of forty-five men, and on May
14, 1804, they left St. Charles, Missouri (now part of the greater metro St.
Louis area). The mission of this "Corps of Discovery" was to find an inland
waterway to the Pacific. The expedition purchased a keelboat, made at
the boatyard of William Greenough of Pittsburgh, Pennsylvania, a claim
disputed by the town of Elizabeth, Pennsylvania, which insists it was built by
one of its residents, Captain John Walker.

After a year and a half, the expedition reached the mouth of the Columbia
River, finding a route to the Pacific. But it was not the envisioned Northwest
Passage that would enable trade and commerce. The group returned to St.

A full-size replica (bisected) of a keelboat at the Lewis and Clark State Historical Site in Hartford, Illinois (across the Mississippi from St. Louis), 2019.

Louis on September 23, 1806. Clark is buried in Bellefontaine Cemetery, befittingly on a hill overlooking the Mississippi River.

Growth was slow during this early period, since it was so difficult to get to the frontier. Prior to the arrival of the steamboat, goods were floated downriver on boats or rafts propelled by the current and guided by large oars. On arrival, they were broken up in New Orleans. Rowers were often new immigrants from Europe. When new settlements in the South were established on the Mississippi, a top priority was for new landowners and their enslaved persons to fell trees and square timbers to be sawed into boards for rafts. Many settlers built water-powered sawmills, and large quantities of lumber were rafted down the river to New Orleans, then loaded onto seagoing vessels bound for the East Coast, the West Indies and other locations.

Going upriver was an arduous task. Early French trappers used a pirogue, carved from the trunk of a tree like a dugout, and two were strapped together with planks on top. Gaps were filled with clay or gum resin. A more refined version was the French batteau (simply the French word for *boat*). Boats would be paddled or poled up the river. Poling involves standing in a boat and using a long pole to push off against the bottom of the river, thereby moving the boat forward.

As payloads increased, merchants developed a keelboat, a flat-bottom boat that drew only two feet. They were between forty and sixty feet long and of ribbed construction. Teams of several men poled up the river using eight-foot poles with iron tips. Using this method, a boat could travel from eight to ten miles upriver a day. In some locations, they could be pulled upstream by ropes tied to horses or mules. The trip from New Orleans to St. Louis on a keelboat took about three months.

There were some ingenious souls who developed "team boats," essentially small paddlewheel vessels powered by horse or mule. In 1826, a Timothy Flint wrote that it was common to see flat-bottom boats using a "bucket-wheel" powered by horses. Most often, these contraptions were used to cross the Mississippi, not go up it. In Missouri, team ferries operated in New Haven, Waverly and St. Mary from the 1880s to as late as 1910. One man, Fortesque Cumming, made a trip down the Mississippi in a keelboat with six horses going around in a circle to power a device.

While Robert Fulton is credited with building the first steamboat, in 1807, the first steamboat did not appear on the Mississippi until 1811—the *New Orleans*—enabling much larger and heavier cargos to move upstream more quickly. In 1817, the first paddleboat arrived in St. Louis, the *Zebulon M. Pike* (named after the man who gave his name to Pikes Peak, Colorado). The modus operandi was for steamships to sail finished goods up the Mississippi and raw materials down. Then, tall-masted seagoing vessels sailed from New Orleans to the Eastern Seaboard or Europe.

Once steamboats proved their effectiveness, there was a massive move to build them and begin using them to haul goods upriver. In 1814, there were only 21 steamboats at New Orleans; in 1828, more than 1,200 cargo steamboats were unloaded. Estimates vary greatly, but by the middle of the century, from 2,500 to 5,000 steamboats a year arrived at St. Louis. As the number of ships increased, prices fell dramatically. This fueled more westward migration and more shipments from the frontier to the East Coast down the river. With time, better and safer steam engines and vessel designs made transport even more efficient.

For some St. Louisans, the Mississippi had nothing to do with commerce. In 1847, the Missouri General Assembly passed an act making it illegal to teach African Americans. To bypass the law, a local Black minister named John Berry Meachum created a school for Blacks on a riverboat in the Mississippi called the Floating Freedom School. Boundary waterways were under federal, not state, jurisdiction.

Meachum's wife, Mary, was an active member of the Underground Railroad. On May 21, 1855, she was caught attempting to smuggle a group of slaves across the Mississippi to Illinois, where slavery was outlawed. For this act, she was criminally charged. She was acquitted of one charge, and the other charges were dropped.

A group of settlers and a Native American watch the SS *Zebulon M. Pike*, the first steamboat to reach St. Louis, on August 2, 1817. *Missouri History Society.*

In 1861, at the height of this massive movement of goods and people, the Civil War began, severely disrupting the river trade as both sides vied for control. Wooden vessels were highly vulnerable to artillery (on ship and on the shore), and the Confederate navy created the first ironclad vessels to resist gunshot. This triggered a naval gunship race between both sides to produce more of these beasts to defeat and control the others and, consequently, to control the trade routes (see chapter "Civil War Ironclads of James Eads").

It was on the Mississippi immediately following the Civil War that the United States suffered the worst maritime disaster in its history, the explosion of the side-wheel steamboat *Sultana*. At war's end, thousands of Union prisoners of war were in Confederate camps awaiting repatriation.

In an effort to make a massive profit, the captain of the *Sultana* left St. Louis and picked up over 2,000 wounded, sick and hungry soldiers from Vicksburg, Mississippi, cramming them on the ship built to carry 376. En route to Missouri, on April 27, 1865, three of the ship's four boilers exploded seven miles upriver from Memphis, and it burned and sank. An estimated 1,700 crewmembers and passengers died, more than during the 1912 sinking of the *Titanic*.

MOTORDROME/MURDERDROME
AT PRIESTER'S PARK

*A*round 1910 at Grand and Meramec, an amusement park called Priester's Park was built. Its star attraction was the St. Louis Motordrome, a wooden arena for racing early motorcycles. It had a circular quarter-mile track banked at an amazing sixty-two degrees, the steepest in the history of motorcycle track racing. The track was composed of two-by-fours, resulting in the name "board track racing." It was extremely dangerous, and the press soon began referring to it as the "Murderdrome." This charming nickname comes from the fact that the bikes attained speeds of almost one hundred miles an hour and were

Crowd seated at the wooden racetrack at Priester's Park, 1914. *St. Louis Mercantile Library*.

not equipped with brakes. Constructed by Jack Prince, this motordrome was part of the FAM American League Circuit. The stadium had room to seat ten thousand people with standing room for thousands more.

Equally interesting, Priester's Park also originated hot-air balloon racing in St. Louis—the genesis of the famous Forest Park Balloon Race. The photo shows the steeply angled track.

SOUTH GRAND BOULEVARD AND MERAMEC STREET, ST. LOUIS, MISSOURI 63116

MOUNDS OF NATIVE AMERICANS

Right across the Mississippi River from St. Louis is the site of Cahokia, which in the twelfth century had a population greater than that of London. The Algonquian-speaking pre-Columbian society spread from the South through the Midwest up to Minnesota. While Cahokia was just a few miles east of St. Louis, the present site of St. Louis is in the center of their civilization's location.

In this era, Native people lived primarily in small villages that dotted the rivers. Unlike nomadic nations that migrated along with food sources, the residents of Cahokia were a settled people with agriculture, skilled trades, hunting and fishing, pottery, carving, copper smelting, astronomy and religion. They traded with other Native people up and down the Mississippi.

The people of Cahokia differed from those of other nations in that they established this major permanent urban area, unknown elsewhere north of Mexico. Unlike other Native pyramid builders, who built with stone, the Cahokia built earthen mounds. The city contained about 120 mounds of varying sizes, of which 81 have survived. The people lived in this area from about 700 to 1400 CE and formed the largest permanent concentration of people in North America north of the Aztecs.

The biggest mound is the largest man-made earthen mound on the North American continent. It is historically referred to as Monks Mound (getting its name from the group of Trappist monks who lived nearby). This mound served religious purposes by elevating the chiefs higher toward the sun god. The mound is one hundred feet tall, covers fourteen

The Big Mound during destruction, 1869. *Missouri Historical Society.*

acres at its base and has a volume of fifty-five million cubic feet of earth in four terraced levels. During construction, the earth was carried in woven baskets, one basket at a time. Archaeology indicates that the mound was topped with a wooden structure. It is speculated to have been a temple or the dwelling of the chief/priest.

Around 1400, about one hundred years before the arrival of Europeans, the civilization dissolved, and there is little agreement about the precise reason or reasons—resource depletion, soil depletion, overfishing, disease or perhaps internal strife. Since the Cahokia people left no written records, we are left to examine what they left behind and to speculate.

The Cahokia civilization existed on the western side of the Mississippi as well. There was once a large mound at what is now the intersection of Broadway and Mound Street, roughly 150 feet long and 30 feet tall. As St. Louis expanded, by 1870 the city had decided to remove the mound. Most of the clay was used to make bricks for buildings. A marker on a granite boulder remains at the site, immediately south of the Stan Musial Veterans Memorial Bridge.

Of the approximately forty other mounds that once existed in St. Louis, only one remains: Sugarloaf Mound. It is the oldest human-made structure in the city. There used to be a house on it, but the Osage Nation bought the property in 2009 and demolished the house in 2017 with an eye on preserving this last piece of Native history. Today, the Cahokia area in Illinois is known as the Cahokia Mounds State Historic Site and is a National Historic Landmark as well as a UNESCO World Heritage Site.

BIG MOUND MARKER, NORTH BROADWAY AND MOUND STREET, ST. LOUIS, MISSOURI 63102

SUGARLOAF MOUND, 4420 OHIO AVENUE, ST. LOUIS, MISSOURI 63111

NATION'S FIRST LYNCHING

Francis McIntosh

*W*here was the site of the nation's first lynching? It was St. Louis. It took place on April 28, 1836, involving a free mixed-race steamboat steward named Francis McIntosh.

McIntosh was taken into custody by a pair of policemen. While he was in their custody, there was a struggle, during which McIntosh killed one of the officers. McIntosh was locked in a cell, and a group of white men dragged him out, took him to North Seventh and Chestnut Streets, tied him to a tree and burned him alive.

Many of the participants were well known, but no one was indicted for the murder. "An investigation into the murder, headed by [aptly named]

A group of white men stand in front of Lynch's Slave Market at 104 Locust Street, St. Louis, 1852. *Missouri Historical Society*.

Judge Luke Lawless, was completely biased, and Lawless even instructed the grand jury not to indict anyone."

The instigator was Bernard M. Lynch, a notorious slave trader who had a slave market at 104 Locust Street. Enslaved persons arrived in the United States in New Orleans, were transferred to steamboats and were brought upriver to St. Louis. Once here, they were offloaded like cargo and herded to slave houses. Lynch has the dubious distinction of lending his name to the terms *lynching* and *lynch mob* when referring to the hanging or killing of an individual without trial or even accusation.

From 1882 to 1968, there were a total of 3,446 lynchings of Black people in the United States, and the vast majority took place in the South. In case you were wondering, Missouri has had fifty-three lynchings of Black people.

Today, the location is the site of a Hooters.

NORTH SEVENTH AND CHESTNUT STREETS, ST. LOUIS, MISSOURI 63101

NEITHER SNOW NOR RAIN

*A*long with its role in moving goods and people from east to west, St. Louis was a case study in the evolution of communication. In the earliest days, the Spanish and French relied on the most rudimentary of messaging—carrying by hand (via rider or canoe) written correspondence from the Crown or governors to other authorities, as well as between business and trade communications. This was the same pace that news traveled since the invention of writing. It was clearly advantageous to communicate more quickly, so the next two hundred years marked steady progress in how we communicate.

In 1785, Congress authorized the use of stagecoaches to deliver mail. Improvements to route planning and efficiency resulted in improved delivery times; by 1822, a letter from Washington, D.C., to Nashville took only eleven days.

With the advent of steamboats, private companies began hauling mail, which took business away from the Post Office Department. To reduce losses, Congress made it illegal for private express companies to carry mail. The Post Office then contracted directly with steamboats by the end of the 1820s on the East Coast. Once steamboats had reached the Mississippi, they, too, began hauling mail. These boats had a life expectancy of just five to six years because of the danger of explosion, fire, collisions and submerged logs.

At the conclusion of the Mexican-American War in February 1848, California became a U.S. territory, and the U.S. Postmaster established a

The *Kate Adams*, built in 1882, a U.S. Mail steamboat, moves on the Mississippi River. *National Postal Museum.*

U.S. Post Office there. By December, steamships under contract with the navy began carrying mail from New York to California via an overland route at the Isthmus of Panama. Mail was unloaded and transported by canoe or pack animal (and years later by train), then put aboard another steamboat headed up the West Coast. The goal was to make the trip in three to four weeks, but it often took up to six weeks. This lengthy period put increased demands on developing an overland route through the continent.

Over the next several years, Congress appropriated funding for several overland routes. But these were slow and dangerous overland routes. Another option of great notoriety appeared, the Pony Express, which could deliver a letter in half the time as previous overland means—just ten days from St. Joseph, Missouri (west of St. Louis) to Sacramento, California. However, it cost five dollars for a half ounce, as opposed to ten cents via the U.S. Mail. Because of the high costs, the Pony Express never ran at a profit, and it operated only from April 3, 1860, to October 26, 1861, just eighteen months. This ending date is not arbitrary; it is two days after the transcontinental telegraph line was completed. Nonetheless, the Pony Express relay rider has been etched in the American imagination with fascination, earning a grandiose history far outweighing its actual contribution.

It is important to realize that until 1863, "mail" meant delivery from one post office to another. That is, you dropped off your letter at the post office in City A, and it arrived at the post office in City B. Letters were labeled with the recipient's name only. It was not until July 1, 1863, that the postal service

Pony Express rider passing the transcontinental telegraph line—impending doom. *Wikimedia Commons.*

delivered letters to an address—and only in one of several "free cities." For the first time, people had to put a street address on a letter.

This was a defining era in the United States, with the completion of both the transcontinental telegraph (1861) and railroad (1869). By wire, a message was delivered instantly, and a letter could travel from New York to San Francisco in four days. By 1930, more than ten thousand trains moved the mail.

Amid the flurry of solutions to move information more quickly, St. Louis was one of five U.S. cities to develop an underground pneumatic tube mail system, in 1905. It ran between Union Station and the Old Post Office (see chapter "Pneumatic Mail Tube System").

Time to Deliver Mail, New York to San Francisco

1849: ship, steamboat, overland Isthmus of Panama	1 month+
1858: railroad to Missouri, stagecoach	30–35 days
1860: railroad to Missouri, Pony Express rider	13–14 days
1869: transcontinental railroad	7 days
1900: transcontinental railroad	4 days, 10 hours
1906: special through-train	3 days, 37 hours
1921: airplane/railroad	3 days, 11 hours
1924: transcontinental airmail	1 day, 11 hours

Barefoot telegram messenger boy, ten years old, Western Union, 1911. *Library of Congress.*

Another invention employed in communication was the airplane, which was invented in 1903. The first commercial airmail route was established in 1926. Service spread slowly, with St. Louis developing landing strips in what today is Forest Park. None other than Charles Lindbergh piloted aircraft (see chapter "Forest Park's Aviation Field and Lindbergh's Airmail Route").

The telegraph had been a phenomenal advancement, capable of transmitting messages instantly across the country, but it was not without its limitations. Messages had to be coded and decoded, and the sender had to wait for the recipient to receive it and reply. A Scottish American teacher for the deaf, Alexander Graham Bell, improved electronic communication by sending voice over lines and patenting the telephone in 1876.

Bell's invention was nothing short of miraculous, and by 1880, there were more than forty-nine thousand phones in the United States. The network grew, and in 1915, Bell made the first coast-to-coast phone call. The popularity of telephones necessitated a massive infrastructure of telephone poles and lines and exchanges, the development of numbering systems for directing calls and of course a way to bill the calls.

At this point, many readers will remember the numerous, rapid telephone-related innovations: the disappearance of party lines, rotary phones replaced by push-button dials, automation (replacing operators), the first wireless phones (with a docking station), the disappearance of operator-placed long-distance calls and charges for long-distance calls, cell phones and satellites. And, of course, these technologies led to the development of the internet, email, virtual conferencing and streaming video. And there is no end in sight.

ST. LOUIS' CUSTOM HOUSE AND POST OFFICE, 815 OLIVE STREET, ST. LOUIS, MISSOURI 63101

NEW MADRID FAULT AND THE DAY THE MISSISSIPPI RIVER RAN BACKWARD

*T*he New Madrid fault zone is the fifth-most-dangerous fault line in the United States. And it is only 160 miles from St. Louis. The most recent severe quakes occurred over two hundred years ago; they shook more than a million square miles and were felt a thousand miles away. They remain the most powerful earthquakes in the contiguous United States east of the Rocky Mountains in recorded history.

The first quakes occurred on December 16, 1811, and two more took place within a few months. They achieved an estimated magnitude of 7.2–8.2. The intensity was enough to create a "fluvial tsunami" in the Mississippi River, making it run backward for several hours.

At this time, Missouri was still a decade from statehood, the population of the territory was about twenty-one thousand (European) people and there were very few multistory buildings. As such, there were few fatalities and comparably limited property damage. That said, the quakes created landslides that destroyed several communities, including Little Prairie, Missouri.

An underground view of the New Madrid fault line in the Bonne Terre Mine, an hour's drive south of St. Louis.

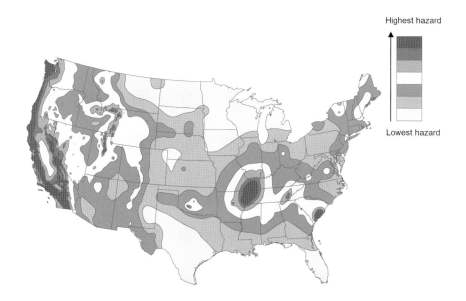

Highest hazard

Lowest hazard

A map by the U.S. Geologic Service outlining areas of seismic activity in the mainland United States, with a large, dark shaded zone immediately south of St. Louis.

To get a firsthand glimpse of the fault line from underground, an hour's drive south of St. Louis is the Bonne Terre Mine. Visitors can see the meeting of the tectonic plates in the ceiling.

Bonus fact: the Mississippi has flowed backward several times: February 1812 (New Madrid earthquake); August 2005 (Hurricane Katrina); August 2012 (Hurricane Isaac) and August 2020 (Hurricane Laura).

1904 WORLD'S FAIR AND THE PYGMY DISPLAYED AT THE NEW YORK BRONX ZOO

*I*n 1904, an African man was bought from slave traders and placed on exhibit at the St. Louis World's Fair and eventually wound up living in a cage with a chimpanzee in the Bronx Zoo Monkey House.

To appreciate the complexity of this story, you need a little backstory. In the 1800s, curiosity shows were wildly popular, bringing exotic animals, oddities and "freaks" to Americans.

These shows sometimes included indigenous people from "primitive" lands, including Australia, Africa and Southeast Asia. They were billed (in the jargon of the day) as "missing links"—"primitive" people who spoke gibberish and wore animal skins as a genetic step between apes and European man.

With the publication of Darwin's *On the Origin of Species*, the scientific community glommed on to the idea that people in technically undeveloped countries were living examples of other hominids rather than *Homo sapiens* with minor genetic adaptations.

To expound on this theory and showcase it during the World's Fair, in March 1904, a former missionary named Samuel Phillip Verner purchased (and technically freed) several "Pygmies" from slave traders in Africa, and he invited them to the United States to become part of an exhibit.

Scientific leaders and anthropologists imported thousands of indigenous peoples from different countries to be exhibited in their traditional clothing and habitats.

Ota Benga at the Bronx Zoo with his chimpanzee companion. *Library of Congress.*

Among the aforementioned races, the Pygmies' habitat was in a little sunken area with a walkway above it, providing the "civilized" white people with a good view of the Africans and their huts. The fair held different events of these people, including the "Grand March of the Barbarians."

Incidentally, the anthropological exhibit featured Native Americans, including the captured legendary Apache warrior Geronimo. For a dime, you could get his autograph. The caption for his photo read, "The Great Apache chieftain, seventy years old but still erect and haughty." He was captured by the U.S. Army in 1886, and for eighteen years he had been their "guest."

The largest exhibit was for the Philippines. Recall that the Philippines was a colony of Spain, the Spanish East Indies, a few years earlier. In 1898, Spain ceded the Philippines to the United States. Yes, the United States, which fought to gain its independence, had itself become a colonial power.

The anthropological exhibits were on the west end of Forest Park. The Philippines sector was just west of what is now Skinker Boulevard.

At the conclusion of the World's Fair in 1905, Verner returned the Pygmies to their homeland. But he convinced one man, Ota Benga, to return to the United States with him, again as a living exhibit. Verner soon began having financial problems, and it was convenient for him to transfer custody of Benga to the American Museum of Natural History in New York City, where Benga would often wander the museum grounds.

After years of living in an environment unnatural to him, Benga became increasingly agitated. At a gathering of wealthy donors, he threw a chair at Florence Guggenheim (of all people), one of the top members of the country's elite. After wearing out his welcome at the museum, Benga had nowhere to

The entrance to Forest Park near the "native habitats," 2020.

go, so provision was made for him to be moved—to New York's Bronx Zoo. Much of the time he wandered around the zoo freely and helped zookeepers, and he spent a great deal of time in the Monkey House with the chimpanzees.

Always open for a new opportunity, zoo administrators came up with a brainstorm: Put a hammock in an empty cage and give Benga a bow and arrow. To spice up the exhibit, zoo officials at the Monkey House exhibited him with an orangutan named Dohong, who would pedal a tricycle around the cage. Ota Benga and Dohong frolicked together, hugging, playing and wrestling.

A local newspaper headline stated, "Bushman Shares a Cage with Bronx Park Apes." Thousands of visitors flocked to see this man in a cage. The *New York Times* wrote the next day, "The joint man-and-monkey exhibition was the most interesting sight in Bronx Park." And zoo attendance (and revenues) increased.

The only ones to complain were the clergy and African American associations. Eventually, public sentiment turned, and the zoo was forced to discontinue the Pygmy exhibit in the Monkey House. Once again, Benga was left to walk the zoo grounds.

That, too, ended with an alleged incident with a knife, and he was moved yet again to a New York orphan asylum and then to a Lynchburg, Virginia seminary. His sad tale ends in 1916, when he committed suicide. And it all began right here in St. Louis.

1904 WORLD'S FAIR FLIGHT CAGE

The Beginning of the St. Louis Zoo

*T*he St. Louis Zoo is recognized as one of the best in the nation. What was the catalyst for the creation of this, the world's first municipally supported zoo?

By 1900, St. Louis was a major transportation and industrial hub, and winning the bid to hold the 1904 World's Fair catapulted it into the global limelight. While many today remember it as the event that introduced the world to the ice cream cone, iced tea, Dr. Pepper, hot dogs and hamburgers, most don't recall that the Flight Cage, now located within the St. Louis Zoo, was built for the fair.

Left: St. Louis Zoo Flight Cage, 2020.

Opposite: The Flight Cage from the 1904 World's Fair. *Missouri History Society*.

The cage was commissioned by the Smithsonian Institution for $17,500, with the intention from the beginning to move it after the World's Fair to the National Zoo in Washington, D.C. In the end, someone did the math regarding the costs for dismantling, shipping and reassembling the giant cage. It was decided that the cage be sold to the City of St. Louis for $3,500.

That was just the cage, empty! The city paid another thirty dollars for four Canadian geese and a pair of Mandarin ducks. (A few owls were donated by area residents.)

With the Flight Cage's purchase, it was not long before someone broached the idea of building a full zoo on the grounds. And, just like that, St. Louis became home to the first municipally supported zoo in the world.

1 GOVERNMENT DRIVE, ST. LOUIS, MISSOURI 63110

1907 BALLOON RACE, GRANDFATHER OF THE GREAT FOREST PARK BALLOON RACE

*O*ne of St. Louis' most popular events is the Great Forest Park Balloon Race, the oldest and most well-attended free hot-air balloon race in the world. In its current form, it originated in 1973 with only six balloons. Over the years, it has grown to over seventy entrants and more than 150,000 spectators. The race itself is preceded by the "Balloon Glow," when the balloons are lighted up at night, providing a delightful visual treat.

The event traces its roots to an internationally famous balloon event, the James Gordon Bennett Cup International Balloon Race, which debuted in St. Louis in October 1907 in Forest Park, sponsored by the Aero Club of America. The entrants included six balloons from Europe (three German, two French, one English) and three from the United States. The event was a distance race, and the victor was German pilot Oscar Erbloch in his balloon *Pommern*, with a distance of 876 miles.

This wasn't St. Louis' only balloon race. The Priester's Park amusement park, which operated the daring Motordrome (see chapter "Motordrome/Murderdrome at Priester's Park"), held the National Elimination Balloon Races in 1914, sponsored by the Aero Club of St. Louis.

This was the era of the aviation craze. Lighter-than-air craft were all the rage, with free-flying balloons and, later, powered craft. (In 1886, Gottlieb Daimler created a sufficiently powerful gasoline engine.) Lighter-than-air

Participants in the James Gordon Bennett Cup International Balloon Race preparing, 1907. *Missouri Historical Society.*

craft reached their pinnacle with large, magnificent dirigibles, epitomized by the *Luftschiff Zeppelin 1*, created by Count Ferdinand von Zeppelin in 1863.

Public enthusiasm never really waned, stoked by progressive milestones such as the Wright brothers and their first controlled heavier-than-air flight in 1903, then by Charles Lindbergh's 1927 solo transatlantic flight from New York to Paris.

Every St. Louisan knows the city's connection to Lindbergh's flight but perhaps not all the details. His trip was promoted by none other than Albert Lambert, who owned Lambert Field, now the city's primary airport, along with other St. Louis businessmen who bankrolled the enterprise. Lindbergh's aircraft, *The Spirit of St. Louis*, was built by the Ryan Aircraft Corporation, which operated the airmail route from St. Louis to Chicago and hired Lindbergh as its chief pilot (see chapter "Forest Park's Aviation Field and Lindbergh's Airmail Route"). The company went on to have its own illustrious career in St. Louis.

NUDE ART THAT
RUFFLED FEATHERS

While most of the Western world has a long history of incorporating the nude human form as a subject in art, St. Louis has exhibited some provincial attitudes. One sculpture created such a stir that it almost sparked an international incident.

The statue commemorates the Germans among the American people (St. Louis had a very significant German population), and it is a memorial to three German American newspapermen. The largest private donor was Adolphus Busch. A selection committee chose the design proposed by Wilhelm Wandschneider from Germany, and upon hearing the news he headed to America to begin the sculpture. When he got off the boat in New York, he was told that Busch had sent him a cable rescinding the award. It turns out the Memorial Association objected to the decision of a nude and forced the selection committee chairman to resign.

Now in New York, Wandschneider went to the German embassy to protest the rescinding of the award after he had been duly selected and had traveled to the United States. The incident almost boiled into an international dispute. Wandschneider apparently smooth-talked the committee, convincing them that the statue of the nude woman itself represented "truth." The association ultimately accepted his design and awarded him the $23,000 prize, and he built the sculpture.

The Naked Truth, Compton Hill Reservoir Park, by Wilhelm Wandschneider, 1914.

As an amusing epilogue, years later, Wandschneider admitted that Busch's cable had in fact arrived as he was leaving Europe, but he destroyed it and acted as if he knew nothing about it. It's an ironic twist, a statue of "Truth" born of a lie.

The original location of *The Naked Truth* was the north end of Reservoir Park. In 1968, the city wanted to build an onramp to I-44 through the area, so the sculpture was moved to its present location in the center of the park, south of the water tower.

THE NAKED TRUTH, COMPTON HILL RESERVOIR PARK, 1700 SOUTH GRAND BOULEVARD, ST. LOUIS, MISSOURI 63104

OLD NEWSBOYS DAY

Dealing with Poverty

hy is there a statue of a paperboy from the early 1900s by the library in the Central West End? This stems from a St. Louis tradition, so for those outside the area, here is the scoop from the beginning. The 1840s brought a large number of immigrants to the United States, and they tended to move to large urban centers such as St. Louis. Families were hard-pressed to earn money, so children were pressed into service in unskilled jobs such as messengers, shoe shiners and newsboys—and the hapless newsboy began to emblemize orphans and poorer families scrambling to earn money.

St. Louis developed an attachment to the newsboys, in part because Lewis Hine, photographer for the National Child Labor Committee, captured on film the suffering and destitution of the city's thousands of waifs—boys as young as five years old hawking papers, huddled up and sleeping on bundles of papers equal to their own size.

The backdrop to the children of our city working to support themselves takes on many forms. The cholera epidemic of 1832, for example, left a significant number of children without caregivers, giving rise to institutions such as the St. Louis Protestant Orphan Asylum, established in 1834.

St. Mary's Orphanage was established in 1843 as a refuge for girls ages five to fourteen. The Great Depression saw many children simply abandoned, as families had no way to care for them. Some children were simply runaways, living on the street or fleeing violent or exploitive environments. This was

Left: Tommy Hawkins, five-year-old newsie, forty inches tall, St. Louis, May 1910. *Library of Congress.*

Below: Protestant Episcopal Orphans Home, Grand Avenue near Lafayette Street, 1873. *Missouri Historical Society.*

an era of extraordinary drunkenness, which often went hand in hand with violence and severe punishment (particularly in Old World families).

A few years later, the Civil War left many families displaced and many men dead, contributing greatly to poverty and the growth in the number of orphans. Mass casualty events such as the Great Cholera Outbreak of 1849 and the Spanish flu of 1918 left innumerable children orphans. In the first ten weeks of the Spanish flu, ten thousand people died in New York City and thirty-one thousand children became orphans. There was no shortage of downtrodden, solitary youth.

In 1906, Father Peter Dunne opened a facility for homeless (abandoned or runaway) and orphaned newsboys, the News Boys Home and Protectorate. This first home was located at 1013 Selby Street. Later that year, it relocated to 2737 Locust Street. The following year, a new home was built at 3010 Washington Avenue. These facilities were for white boys only. It was not until 1931 that a home for Black boys, Father Dunne's Colored Orphans' Home, opened at 3028 Washington Avenue. In 1934, it was relocated to 901 North Garrison, and it closed in 1941.

It is important to understand that the first of these homes opened twenty-three years before the Great Depression; St. Louis was a booming city, and businesses flourished as people, native born and immigrant alike, flocked to the West—the land of opportunity. Yet, at a time when many businesses were flourishing and many men were becoming rich, this became an unprecedented period of hardship for and exploitation of children. Conditions were poor and often hazardous, and the newsies epitomized the lowest rung of society, struggling in an effort to survive.

Old Newsboy statue on Lindell Boulevard, 2020.

Federal legislation was proposed in 1924 to prohibit child labor, but the states did not ratify it. Opponents said it would be detrimental to the economy. It was not until 1938 that the Fair Labor Standards Act was passed. In reality, one of the biggest factors contributing to the elimination of child labor was the

Depression itself. Making it illegal to hire children was primarily an effort to create jobs for desperate unemployed adult workers, not to protect children.

Several years after World War II, in 1957, a local newspaper, the *Globe-Democrat*, decided to start selling a special edition of the newspaper to raise money for local children's charities. Because of the sponsorship by newspapers, the annual event is called Old Newsboys Day.

For five decades, on the Thursday before Thanksgiving, volunteers have stood at key intersections around town to sell newspapers and collect donations. To commemorate the efforts of thousands of volunteers over the years, the Wetterau Family Foundation commissioned this statue, made by Jaye Gregory. The statue's plaque reads: "Donated by the Wetterau Family in Honor of the Old Newsboys Organization Uplifting the Spirit of Over 100,000 St. Louis Children."

OLD NEWSBOYS STATUE, LINDELL BOULEVARD AND YORK AVENUE, ST. LOUIS, MISSOURI 63108

PNEUMATIC MAIL TUBE SYSTEM

*T*here is a long-forgotten two-mile underground mail tube that runs beneath Pine Street. In the nineteenth century, pneumatic tubes were enormously popular as a method for transporting small canisters within large buildings; complex systems of tubes could convey mail within minutes. It was a far more efficient system than pushing mail carts through skyscrapers.

The U.S. Post Office operated large-scale tube systems modeled after those in several major European cities in a handful of U.S. cities: Boston, Brooklyn, Chicago, New York, Philadelphia and St. Louis. The St. Louis system was the smallest, as well as the last one built in the country. The European experience was that the tube system was more efficient than the alternative, using wagons to move the mail. At its peak, New York City's system, the largest in the country, had a whopping fifty-five miles of mail tubes; Chicago had nine miles.

In 1905, St. Louis built its comparatively diminutive two-mile section underneath Pine Street, connecting Union Station, where mail arrived in St. Louis by rail, to the Old Post Office on Ninth Street.

The mail tubes had an internal diameter of eight inches, and the mail capsules were seven inches in diameter and twenty-two inches long. The cylinders held approximately six hundred standard letters. A system of pumps and fans blew or sucked the capsules at about thirty miles per hour.

Unfortunately, the system did not work all that well. It slowed due to several reasons, and it ruined a lot of mail. More important, the introduction

New York Post Office pneumatic tube, 1912. *Library of Congress*.

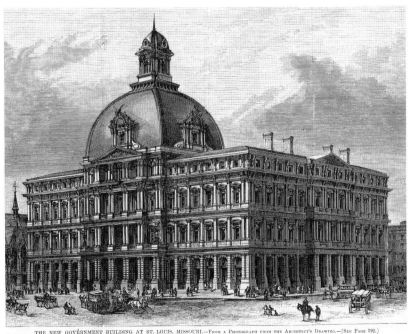

THE NEW GOVERNMENT BUILDING AT ST. LOUIS, MISSOURI.—FROM A PHOTOGRAPH FROM THE ARCHITECT'S DRAWING.—[SEE PAGE 392.]

Custom House and Post Office, between Eighth and Ninth and Olive and Locust. *Missouri Historical Society*.

of the automobile spelled economic death for the tubes. The system cost about $17,000 per mile annually to maintain, and St. Louis had four miles (two miles both ways), amounting to $68,000 a year (in 1905 dollars).

Trucks could carry a lot of mail quickly, cheaply and reliably—and without ruining it. And soon the system had been phased out.

In essence, it was a parallel tale to the Pony Express (which, despite the popularity of the myth, operated for just eighteen months), the eastern end of which originated in St. Joseph, Missouri, about three hundred miles west of St. Louis.

Undoubtedly, the tubes are still beneath Pine Street, but who knows what became of the stations on either end? The technology is still used today at drive-throughs in banks and pharmacies.

Some interesting side notes: In New York City, a test canister was sent carrying a black cat. The men who launched the canisters were called "Rocketeers." And in New York City, a man ran a pilot program to transport people, much like a subway, via pneumatic power.

ST. LOUIS' CUSTOM HOUSE AND POST OFFICE, 815 OLIVE STREET,
    ST. LOUIS, MISSOURI 63101

PROHIBITION ENDS
BY REDEFINING ALCOHOL

*P*rohibition was an ill-thought solution to the national catastrophe of chronic alcohol abuse. If you want a good read, study what "heavy drinking" used to be and its accompanying utter ruin of families, marriages and lives on a national level. It makes today's drug crisis look like a kindergarten party. If there is any defense of the Prohibition movement, it was that America's alcohol abuse and addiction problem was so horrific that it called for drastic measures.

Prohibition was a solution borne out of desperation to regulate those who refused to regulate themselves. It was furiously debated in Congress and was widely unpopular. That by itself should tell you how bad the problem was. Unfortunately, and to nobody's surprise, the immediate consequence of Prohibition was a boom in organized crime. In addition to the abuse of legal medicinal and religious applications of alcohol (a lot of people must have started taking personal communion), illegal supplies flourished.

Bootleg stills popped up, rumrunners smuggled booze from Canada and the hot rod was invented to run moonshine as cars were souped up to outrun police. (The term *souped up* originated in 1911, when people injected narcotics into horses to make them run faster.) These cars were the origin of today's NASCAR. At every level, underground alcohol flourished: distilling, transportation and retailing (see chapter "Whiskey Milking Scandal").

Above: Adolphus Busch III, August Busch Sr. and August Busch Jr. pose with the first case of post-Prohibition beer. August Busch Sr. holds an envelope addressed to the White House. *Missouri Historical Society*.

Left: Today, you can still go through the secret door in the floor behind the bar at the Corner Bar in St. Charles. It is the second-oldest bar in Missouri, 2020.

Prohibition led to the creation of the speakeasy, so named because people would only discuss them under their breath. A surviving example is the Corner Bar in St. Charles, the second-oldest bar in the state (opened in 1865). There is a secret door in the floor behind the bar and a staircase leading to the secret drinking area—and a bowling alley! It is the nation's only remaining "cocked hat" bowling alley. The sport derives its name from the way bowlers wore their derbies while playing. It has narrow lanes and small balls (compared to standard bowling). This venue can be rented out for parties.

From 1920 to 1933, crime worsened, and the general public was tired of not being able to drink—at all. In 1933, Congress started the process to repeal Prohibition, a process that would take months. In an effort to hasten the law's departure, congressmen did what all politicians do: make another law to subvert the first law.

Congress simply redefined "intoxicant" to allow beer with 3.2 percent alcohol content. It is a similar concept to how companies can legally claim their yogurt is organic or their bread is all natural while containing chemicals and additives.

In St. Louis, at midnight on April 7, 1933, the Anheuser-Busch and Falstaff breweries were mobbed by happy crowds. At Lindell west of North Grand, Mayor-Elect Bernard Dickmann led the first round for the crowd at the Elks Club, in what today is the parking lot west of Jesuit Hall at Saint Louis University.

A huge party with six hundred people was held in the posh Hotel Jefferson on North Tucker. The hotel was built in 1904 to serve visitors to the Louisiana Purchase Exposition. It was overhauled in the 1920s to include a two-story art deco ballroom with balconies and a massive chandelier. Sadly, the ballroom was walled up in the 1970s.

ELKS CLUB (NOW JESUIT HALL), 3601 (OR 3617) LINDELL BOULEVARD, ST. LOUIS, MISSOURI 63108

CORNER BAR, 571 FIRST CAPITOL DRIVE, ST. CHARLES, MISSOURI 63301

HOTEL JEFFERSON, TWELFTH STREET (NOW TUCKER BOULEVARD) AT LOCUST STREET, ST. LOUIS, MISSOURI 63101

RACE RIOTS OF EAST ST. LOUIS, 1917

From July 1 to 3, 1917, East St. Louis was the site of one of the nation's most horrifying mob riots. Just three months after the nation entered World War I, there were three straight days of continuous violence against the African Americans of East St. Louis. In that period, angry whites attacked African Americans at random. The official record states that thirty-nine Black men, women and children and nine whites were killed (unofficial estimates are much higher). Mobs burned and destroyed much of the Black neighborhoods, resulting in $400,000 (1917 dollars) in property damage.

The spark igniting this violence was a drive-by shooting. On July 1, an unknown white man drove through a Black neighborhood and shot into Black residents' homes. Intent on defending themselves, a group of Black men got weapons, and when another car with two white men drove by, the Black men shot and killed the men in the car. It was a grave mistake; the two men were police officers en route to investigate the drive-by shooting. This was the kerosine poured on the spark.

By the morning of July 2, news had spread about Black men shooting two white police officers, and throngs of whites began a rampage. For two days, they randomly beat Black persons. On the third, a group of whites ambushed Black workers as they left their factory jobs. The rioters indiscriminately beat, shot and lynched any Black person they came across.

People attempted to flee town, some by crossing the bridge into Missouri. The police closed the bridge, leaving people trapped on the Illinois side.

Constable on a horse during the East St. Louis race riots. *Missouri Historical Society.*

Frantic, some made makeshift rafts out of logs, old doors or debris or tried to swim. Many drowned in the process. Of the town's twelve thousand Black citizens, more than half made their way out. To regain control, the National Guard was called in.

After the third day, the violence subsided. Once the dust settled, people wanted answers. Local authorities conducted investigations, leading to indictments against 105 people. But only 20 white rioters received prison sentences for the killings and the destruction.

Congress conducted an investigation and released a report in July 1918. The report cited many factors, one being unions retaliating against Blacks for taking white jobs. In the spring of 1917, the predominantly white workers at the Aluminum Ore Company went on strike; the recent migration of Blacks from the South provided a ready-made labor pool, which plainly angered the strikers and the union.

In the end, the congressional report summarized that East St. Louis' government was corrupt and its police force incompetent. It also concluded that labor conflict was a factor but that the primary factor was racial animosity.

The 1917 riots were the largest race riots in the country to date, but they would soon be surpassed on a grand scale with the Tulsa race riots in 1921. During two days of rioting, whites destroyed Tulsa's prosperous Greenwood District, known as Black Wall Street. The rioting was based on allegations that a Black man had attempted to rape a white woman. Before any investigations could be made, whites burned and destroyed thirty-five blocks of the district. Three hundred people died, and another eight hundred were injured. The Red Cross reported that the riots left ten thousand Tulsa residents homeless and calculated property damage in the tens of millions of dollars (in today's dollars). During the riots, six airplanes circled the area and dropped nitroglycerin on buildings, blowing them up and igniting them. Years later, CBS News reported that, "The first time Americans were terrorized by an aerial assault was not Pearl Harbor" but Tulsa.

REINTERMENT OF THE DEAD

With so much going on above the ground in St. Louis, we often do not focus on the incredible history of those people beneath it. The burial of the dead has usually been restricted to the outskirts of towns, but as populations grow, cemeteries inevitably find themselves enveloped by towns as they grow into cities. In early St. Louis, the outskirts of town were marked by Lemay Ferry Road, St. Charles Rock Road and Gravois Road.

Early on, cemeteries faced the problem of burial of the dead during mass casualty events. During the 1849 cholera epidemic, in a period of three months, about 10 percent of the population died. In April 1849, 120 died of cholera. On July 18, there were 88 burials in a single day. The highest death rates were north and south of present-day downtown (the slums), where the poor simply buried their dead in ditches. Official figures are now assumed to be low because of the era and because some people from St. Louis were often buried outside the city.

The threat was so severe that on May 4, the city took over Arsenal Island (four miles south of downtown) and renamed it Quarantine Island. (Some sources state it was two different islands.) Incoming ships were inspected, and those persons with symptoms were quarantined there until they recovered or died (three guesses about the likely outcome).

The dead were buried in a graveyard on the island. During the Civil War, two thousand Confederate soldiers were buried here with wooden crosses. In the 1860s, flooding swept away most of the markers, and most graves were

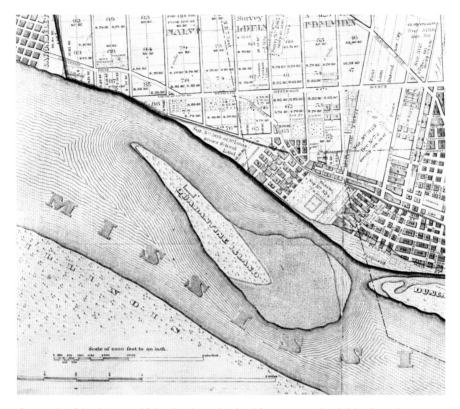

Quarantine Island (Arsenal Island), where the dead from quarantined ships from the 1849 cholera epidemic were buried. Two thousand Confederate dead were buried here during the Civil War. In the 1860s, the island flooded, removing markers, and graves were relocated to Jefferson Barracks Cemetery. *Missouri Historical Society.*

relocated to Jefferson Barracks Cemetery, marked "Unknown," because their markers had washed away.

At the end of the epidemic, in 1850, St. Louis created the city death register. After a second cholera epidemic in 1866 (smaller than in 1849, killing only 3,500), the city established the St. Louis Board of Health, which established sanitary regulations. In 1878, the city passed an ordinance closing all city cemeteries. Even the most established graveyards had to move. The Old Cathedral moved most of its graves to Calvary Cemetery, and many others were reinterred several times from old city cemeteries, and, unfortunately, over the years many were lost.

Some cemeteries have been relocated over time because they simply outgrew their capacity. Nobody could have imagined how big the city would grow.

Nazareth Cemetery, founded in 1874, held as many as 20,000 graves. The graves have been reinterred elsewhere to build the Nazareth Nursing Home. About 1,200 of the graves held the early members of the Sisters of St. Joseph of Carondelet. These were relocated to Resurrection Cemetery in Southwest St. Louis County.

In 1849, Bellefontaine Cemetery was founded in part because so many other cemeteries closed or moved. From 1849 to 1851, about half of its burials were reinterments.

In recent years, reinterments have been due largely to development projects. In some instances, cemeteries are very small and construction proceeded around them. You would never know it, but the very busy intersection of 141 and Olive is home to the one-and-a-half-acre Arminia Lodge Cemetery. It was established in 1884 by the Arminia Lodge No. 374 of the Deutsch Order of Harugari, a German fraternal organization.

Rather than cemeteries being relocated due to outgrowing the property, many more recent relocations are due to development. Such was the case with the Washington Park Cemetery. Established in 1920 in what today is the City of Berkeley, its seventy-five acres were designated as a Black cemetery. Over time, it became the largest Black cemetery in St. Louis.

In the late 1950s, the city disinterred thousands of graves to build Interstate 70 through the middle of the cemetery. (One source claimed some bodies were actually paved over, but I found no corroborating records.)

In 1972, another nine acres of Washington Park were claimed, this time for Lambert International Airport. It happened again in 1996 for expansion of the airport's longest runway.

On yet another occasion, in 1992, land was acquired for the Metrolink extension, and between 11,974 and 13,600 souls were relocated to about twenty area cemeteries. Sadly, burial records of many of the moves were mishandled, and many families lost track of grave locations.

The most recent iteration of St. Louis' Old Cathedral was completed in 1834. The old graves from the original cemetery were moved long ago.

THE REVOLUTIONARY WAR BATTLE
IN ST. LOUIS

*I*f Missouri was not part of the United States, how could St. Louis be the site of a battle during the American Revolutionary War? This is an odd tale about the War of Independence battle in which British and Native Americans attacked a French trading post led by Spanish lieutenant governor Fernando de Leyba in a single stone tower.

At the time of this battle, most people living in St. Louis were French; it was a vital trading center with Native Americans across the Mississippi. The British wanted control of the city to damage the economy of the rebels, and the Spanish also had a presence here. Anticipating a British incursion, they planned for a stone fort with four towers, but they were only able to construct one before the battle.

The Battle of St. Louis (or Battle of San Carlos) took place on May 28 (or May 26, depending on the source), 1770, near present-day Walnut Street and Broadway. In fact, Walnut Street was originally named Rue de la Tour (French for "Tower Road," in reference to the stone tower of the Spanish fort). Today, you can see a plaque in front of the Hilton St. Louis at South Broadway and Walnut.

This location is home to yet another piece of Spanish history: the Spanish Pavilion. The lower section of the Hilton at this location is a relocated building from the 1964 World's Fair in New York, the Spanish Pavilion. While serving at the World's Fair, it housed a 780-seat theater, three restaurants and exhibition halls filled with Spanish artifacts and art, including paintings by Spanish masters El Greco, Goya, Velázquez and Picasso.

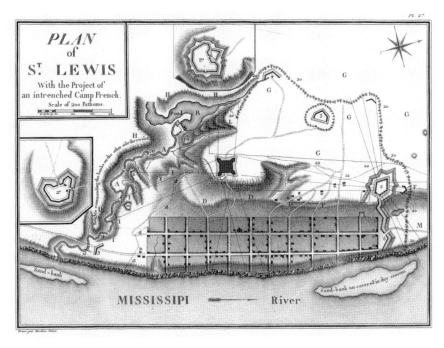

Above: A 1796 French map of St. Louis by Georges-Henri-Victor Collot indicating the location of Fort San Carlos (dark square object in center), the only notable military fortification of the area. *Library of Congress*.

Left: The replica of the *Santa Maria* from the New York World's Fair next to the Arch. *Missouri Historical Society*.

When the 1964 World's Fair was over, the mayor of St. Louis, Alfonso Juan Cervantes, of Spanish ancestry, conducted a fundraiser to move the building from New York to St. Louis in 1966. The structure was lavishly appointed with walnut ceiling blocks, Spanish floor tiles, stained glass and beautiful courtyards. It was rebuilt just north of the brand-new Busch Memorial Stadium; as a touching symbol, on October 7, 1966, the government of Spain provided a piece of granite from the tomb of Queen Isabella to serve as the pavilion's cornerstone. The queen, you will recall, had funded the expedition of Italian sailor Cristoforo Colombo, or in Spanish, Cristóbal Colón, to the Indies.

The Spanish International Pavilion opened on May 25, 1969, and a year later, on June 15, 1970, it filed bankruptcy. It later became a Marriott and is now the Hilton–St. Louis at the Ballpark.

As a final sad note to an already sad tale, to boost publicity for the Spanish Pavilion, Mayor Cervantes got some of his supporters to purchase an eighty-foot replica of Columbus's ship *Santa Maria* from the New York World's Fair for $375,000. It was brought by tug up the Mississippi, and on June 28, 1969, a violent storm passed through the city with seventy-mile-per-hour winds, tearing the ship from its moorings. It was blown two miles downstream and struck a dock on the east bank of the river and sank. Workers raised it, but the ship had a massive hole torn in the side, so it met with an unceremonious demise.

HILTON–ST. LOUIS AT THE BALLPARK, 1 SOUTH BROADWAY, ST. LOUIS, MISSOURI 63102

REVOLUTIONARY WAR SUNKEN
BRITISH NAVAL ARTILLERY

*W*here in St. Louis can you find three naval artillery pieces from a British vessel sunk just weeks before the signing of the Declaration of Independence? Lafayette Park.

In June 1776, just weeks before the Continental Congress approved the Declaration of Independence, a British Coventry Class (or Enterprise Class, depending on source) frigate, the HMS *Actaeon*, ran aground and could not be refloated, so it was set on fire by its crew to avoid capture. Americans boarded the ship and captured trophies before it was lost. The ship had a brief career, having been built only one year earlier. Its heavy armament

British Revolutionary War cannons in Lafayette Park, circa 1897–1920. *Missouri Historical Society.*

The same artillery pieces today: two "Long Toms" (*outside*) and a "Carronade" (*center*) gun from the British frigate HMS *Actaeon* recovered off the coast of Charleston Harbor.

included twenty-four "9-pounder" guns and four "3-pounder" guns (so named by the weight of the shot).

An account is recorded on a plaque:

> *These guns are from the British Man of War "Acteon"* [sic] *sunk in an attack on Sullivan's Island in Charleston Harbor S.C. June 28, 1776. In 1887 a British vessel entering Charleston Harbor ran upon an obstruction which proved to be the forgotten guns of the "Acteon."* [sic] *They were raised and sold at auction and they were bought by the Missouri Commandery of the military Order of the Loyal Legion and presented to Lafayette Park October 20, 1897.*

Curiously, the plaque misspells the name of the vessel (which is *Actaeon*).

LAFAYETTE PARK, 2023 LAFAYETTE AVENUE, ST. LOUIS, MISSOURI 63104

REYNARD THE FOX

*H*ave you ever noticed the several statues in St. Louis of a fox wearing clothes, gnawing on a drumstick and drinking from a stein? Here are three photos of statues that appear on the corner of the Anheuser-Busch bottling facility, a pair at the gate of Kingsland Court and a pair on the roof of Hodak's. The root of the story goes back to Anheuser-Busch and Prohibition.

Founded in 1852, brewer Anheuser-Busch is an inseparable part of St. Louis history. A pivotal point in its history occurred in 1929 during Prohibition, which forced the end of beer production. Grappling with the reality of complying with the law while remaining in business, the brewery decided to switch all production to a non-alcoholic malt beverage called Bevo. Bevo actually was not created *because* of Prohibition. A-B began making it in 1916, when the U.S. Army banned alcohol. Since A-B already had a formula and marketing in place, it was simply a matter of transitioning from beer products to Bevo. The name *Bevo* itself was fabricated from the word *beverage* and the Slavic word for beer, *pivo*, and was pronounced "bee-vo" (although, alternatively, I've heard it is correctly pronounced "beh-vo").

Which brings us to the revelation of Reynard the Fox. The character comes from French stories from the Middle Ages and, thus, would have been known to European immigrants of the time. The anthropomorphic fox was selected as the mascot of Anheuser-Busch and appeared on the label and all marketing.

Above, left: Reynard the Fox, Arsenal Street and South Broadway.

Above, right: Reynard the Fox, 3600 Kingsland Court.

Left: Reynard the Fox, Gravois and McNair Avenues.

After years of Prohibition, people were not willing to do without alcohol, and bootleg alcohol was introduced by organized crime. Way to go, puritans. With steady streams of illegal alcohol flowing in, demand for legal Bevo fell off, and A-B stopped production in 1929, four years before the end of Prohibition in 1933.

ARSENAL STREET AND SOUTH BROADWAY, ST. LOUIS, MISSOURI 63118
3600 KINGSLAND COURT, ST. LOUIS, MISSOURI 63111
GRAVOIS AND McNAIR AVENUES, ST. LOUIS, MISSOURI 63104

THE RUINS AT
TOWER GROVE PARK

Most residents have seen, visited or at least heard of "The Ruins" in Tower Grove Park. But few are familiar with the backstory. The land for the park was donated by none other than Henry Shaw (of Missouri Botanical Garden fame), and he sought some ancient artifacts to make this space more interesting.

Opposite: The ruins of the Lindell Hotel at Sixth Street and Washington after the fire of March 30, 1867. *Missouri Historical Society*.

Above: Part of "The Ruins" in Tower Grove Park, 2020.

In 1867, a fire broke out in the beautiful luxury Lindell Hotel downtown. Shaw rescued a large number of the burned limestone blocks and columns, which gave the effect of ancient ruins. The ruins underwent a restoration in 2010 by Emerson and other park supporters, and it has remained one of the city's most popular spots.

TOWER GROVE PARK, 4257 NORTHEAST DRIVE, ST. LOUIS, MISSOURI 63110
LINDELL HOTEL (ORIGINAL LOCATION), SIXTH STREET AND WASHINGTON, ST. LOUIS, MISSOURI 63010

SAVING THE VINEYARDS
OF FRANCE FROM EXTINCTION

*T*his chapter recounts St. Louis' role in helping to save Europe's wine-growing industry from absolute destruction.

A small insect, *Grape phylloxera*, native to the eastern half of the United States, managed to get transported from the Midwest to Europe in the 1850s. It was introduced by an English botanist who collected specimens of American vines.

In a classic case of a non-indigenous species wreaking havoc in a new ecosystem, in only fifteen years, the insect had devastated 40 percent of French grapevines, feeding on the grape plants' roots and killing them. French vineyards today produce over forty billion bottles of wine a year.

The extremely small, pale-yellow, sap-sucking insects feed on the roots and leaves of grapevines. The insects deform the roots and create a fungus that cuts the flow of water and nutrients to the vine.

The infestation was so broad and severe that the wine-growing vines of France and other places in Europe were destined to be eradicated. Varieties that had been painstakingly cultivated for hundreds of years risked being lost forever.

The first to identify the lifecycles of the *Grape phylloxera* as the cause of the plants' destruction were Dr. George Engelmann, the first botanist at the Missouri Botanical Garden, and Charles Riley, the Missouri state entomologist.

After they identified and studied the problem, Engelmann and Riley's solution was to graft the top part of surviving European grapevines (called

Right: Dr. George Engelmann, the first botanist at the Missouri Botanical Garden, 1881. *Missouri History Society*.

Below: 1909 map showing the spread of *Grape phylloxera* through southern France.

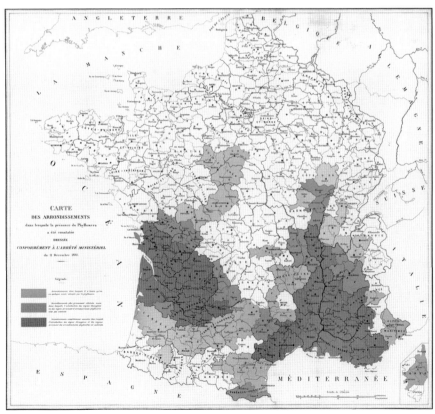

the scion) onto resistant American grapevine rootstock. This would allow the century-old European variety to continue to survive while retaining their delicate European flavors. The wines include Cabernet Sauvignon– and Merlot-driven blends from Bordeaux, Pinot Noir from Burgundy and Cognac.

THE SEARCH FOR PLANET VULCAN

*T*his is not a myth, not a trick, not a tale. This is the bona fide account of the search to discover the elusive planet Vulcan in the late 1800s. *Star Trek* fans, take a sedative.

On January 2, 1860, French astronomer Urbain LeVerrier worked out a formula, based on the observable irregularities in the orbit of Mercury, that indicated the presence of another planet in orbit between Mercury and the sun. He was so sure of his theory that he presented it to the Académie des Sciences in Paris. He named this yet-unseen planet Vulcan, after the Roman god of fire.

Publication of his theory sent ripples through the global scientific community, and the search for proof became an obsession.

Nine years later, Washington University's second chancellor, William Chauvenet, a graduate of Yale, was swept up in the fervor and took up the cause. He pushed for the advancement of astronomy at the university, and astronomers began pursuing solar eclipses, considering these the only opportunities to observe the planet. Despite tremendous effort, the quest was fruitless until 1919, when Einstein's new theory of general relativity was used to explain the irregularities in Mercury's orbit.

Before Chauvenet, in 1857, the university's first chancellor, William Greenleaf Eliot (grandfather of author T.S. Eliot) announced that St. Louis philanthropist James Yeatman had donated $1,500 to make a telescope. In 1863, after becoming chancellor, Chauvenet published his *Treatise on Spherical and Practical Astronomy*, and the same year the university finalized the

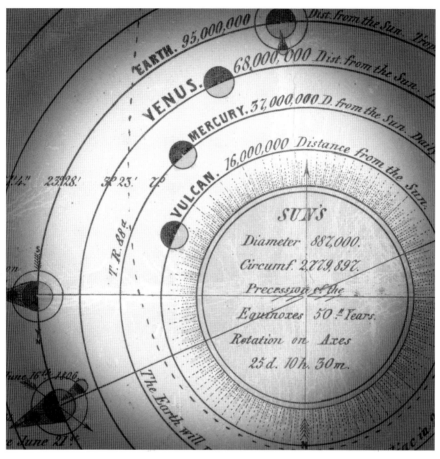

Above: An 1846 map of the solar system, including Vulcan as the planet closest to the sun. *Library of Congress*.

Left: Washington University's Crow Observatory seen from the ground, 2020.

purchase of a six-inch refractor telescope that would come to bear his name: the Yeatman Refractor.

At that time, Washington University (named after George Washington) was downtown, enclosed by Washington Avenue, Lucas Place and Locust Street, and the telescope and observatory were located at Eighteenth and St. Charles Streets.

The university arranged to move into the buildings used during the 1904 World's Fair after it was over, 103 acres west of Forest Park. The observatory was initially relocated to where Louderman Hall now stands, and in 1954, it was relocated again to its current location atop Crow Hall, where it became the Crow Observatory.

And I got all the way through this without making a Spock joke.

CROW OBSERVATORY, WASHINGTON UNIVERSITY DEPARTMENT OF PHYSICS, 1 BROOKINGS DRIVE, ST. LOUIS, MISSOURI 63130

ORIGINAL OBSERVATORY LOCATION: EIGHTEENTH STREET AND ST. CHARLES STREET, ST. LOUIS, MISSOURI 13103

SEEDS FROM SPACE

A Tree Growing in the Botanical Garden

Dubbed one of the "Space Gummies" trees, this tree is one of two that grew from seeds given to the Missouri Botanical Garden that were carried into space aboard the space shuttle *Discovery*.

*O*n August 30, 1984, astronaut Charles Walker was aboard the space shuttle *Discovery* on its maiden voyage. Among his personal effects were two hundred sweet gum tree seeds. They orbited the earth until September 5. After the mission, the seeds were germinated by the U.S. Forest Service in Walker's hometown of Bedford, Indiana. (He had worked for the Forest Service while attending Purdue University.)

Because of his association with the state, Walker donated the majority of the seeds to places in Indiana. His wife, Susan Flowers, was from St. Louis. She was a spokeswoman for McDonnell Douglas (now Boeing) and a former manager of public relations for the Missouri Botanical Garden. She suggested he donate two seeds to both entities, which he did.

The seedlings were nicknamed "Space Gummies." In 1992, the Botanical Garden planted both seeds. Unfortunately, one of their two trees died in 2007. The surviving sweet gum tree stands just west of Henry Shaw's mausoleum, outside the gate.

Somehow, this incredible history became lost in the shuffle, and even though the facts are now known, the saga remains in obscurity.

MISSOURI BOTANICAL GARDEN, 4344 SHAW BOULEVARD, ST. LOUIS, MISSOURI 63110

SOCIAL EVIL HOSPITAL

First U.S. City to Legalize Prostitution

St. Louis was a major military hub during the Civil War, and large concentrations of soldiers invariably come with large armies of prostitutes. The police had great difficulty dealing with it, so civil authorities decided on a different route, following the model of the French, in order to curb the rampant spread of disease. In 1870, the city passed the Social Evil Ordinance, which required women engaging in prostitution to obtain licenses and have routine venereal disease exams.

Yes, St. Louis was the first city in the nation to legalize prostitution. In 1870, there were 5,000 licenses issued. The city's population was 350,000, half of whom were men. So there were 175,000 women, and 40 percent were between the ages of eighteen and forty: 70,000. This means that about 7 percent of women in St. Louis of likely age obtained licenses for prostitution.

There were brothels reported all over town, but workers from poorer neighborhoods worked where the America's Center now stands. And where was the "hot spot"? It was on Almond Street (later renamed Valentine Street), which was later plowed under to make way for the Gateway Arch. Yes, today tourists flock to the city's most famous landmark, unaware the site was a popular place for a different type of tourist attraction.

With all this free enterprise, in September 1872, the city established the Social Evil Hospital to treat venereal disease among prostitutes. It stood at the northwest corner of Arsenal Street and Sublette Avenue.

Female Hospital (Social Evil Hospital), Old Manchester Road at Arsenal Street, 1900.
Missouri Historical Society.

After only four years, the brief flirtation with legal prostitution was over. One can speculate that the Victorian mindset had seen enough sinful behavior. (Of course, it just went back underground.) The hospital was renamed the Female Hospital, tending to venereal disease and serving unmarried expectant mothers.

In 1914, the hospital that once stood at Arsenal and Sublette was demolished and replaced by Sublette Park. Yes, you are playing tennis where the working girls got their checkups.

Thirty years before prostitution was legalized, before the Civil War, one of the most famous madams in the city, Eliza Haycraft, arrived in town. In this era, a single woman's career options were limited to being a housewife, a nurse, a stenographer, a seamstress, a teacher or, all else failing, a prostitute. It was apparently one job unaffected by economic depression.

While she never learned to read or write, Eliza was a savvy and shrewd businesswoman and investor. Over the following thirty years, she became extremely wealthy. Coming from modest stock, she had a delicate spot in her heart for the poor and provided extensive support to the needy.

Eliza Haycraft, famous prostitute and madam during the boom Civil War era, businesswoman and philanthropist—the wealthiest woman in the city in her day. *Missouri Historical Society*.

She died in 1871 (one year after prostitution was legalized) after amassing a quarter of a million dollars in assets, making her the wealthiest woman in the city. She was much loved, yet she was refused burial at Bellefontaine Cemetery. Public pressure was so intense that the cemetery finally agreed to admit her with the provision that no marker be erected. I visited the spot, and indeed, there are no other plots around hers.

SUBLETTE PARK, ARSENAL STREET AND SUBLETTE AVENUE, ST. LOUIS, MISSOURI 63139

SOLDIERS MEMORIAL STATUES AND WORLD WAR II STOLEN ART RETRIEVAL

Sacrifice, one of four larger-than-life statues by Walker Hancock that guard the doors to the Soldiers Memorial in downtown St. Louis, 2020.

*T*he Soldiers Memorial in downtown St. Louis has four large limestone sculptures of people next to giant horses. Titled *Courage*, *Vision*, *Sacrifice* and *Loyalty*, they were created by St. Louis native Walker Hancock, who attended Washington University.

Installed in 1939, the sculptures were part of a Federal Art Project commission. The project, part of the Depression-era New Deal, provided jobs to artists. (Perhaps they should revive this project during today's economic situation). In all, the program was responsible for 17,744 statues and over 2,000 murals nationwide.

During World War II, Hancock was drafted into the army in 1942. He later was informed about the creation of the American Commission for the Protection and Salvage of Artistic and Historic Monuments in Europe. He would become a member of the U.S. Army's Monuments, Fine Arts, and Archives program (MFAA). In this role, he compiled lists of protected monuments for France.

The group of 345 men and women from fourteen nations who served as art historians to find and restore stolen artwork came to be known as the "Monuments Men." They gained renewed interest in 2014 with the release of the film of the same name. (Hancock was played by another St. Louisan, John Goodman.)

Among their many retrievals, Captain Hancock and his team inspected a cache of stolen art in a copper mine near the town of Siegen, Germany, in April 1945. The contents included the relics of Charlemagne from Aachen Cathedral. Hancock and fellow Monuments Man George Stout snuck behind enemy lines while under fire to reach the Aachen treasury. Other notable finds by teams Hancock was on include Michelangelo's *Madonna of Bruges* (Altaussee); van Eyck's *Ghent Altarpiece* (Altaussee) and Manet's *In the Conservatory* (Merkers).

The majority of looted treasures from occupied Europe were found and returned.

As a sidenote, Hancock sculpted the piece *Zuni Bird Charmer* at the St. Louis Zoo.

SOLDIERS MEMORIAL MILITARY MUSEUM, 1315 CHESTNUT STREET, ST. LOUIS, MISSOURI 63103

SPANISH FLU OF 1918

German Spies, Aspirin and Phonograph Records

A mid one of the world's deadliest pandemics of modern times, St. Louis experienced some of the lowest infection and death rates, due to an intelligently planned and aggressive campaign of containment. During World War I, the United States experienced nearly as many deaths due to the Spanish flu as to combat casualties. Globally, the disease infected about a third of the world's population, about 500 million people, of whom about 50 million died, including about 675,000 in the United States. More than two-thirds of the total American casualties died in a single ten-week period in the autumn of 1918.

At the outbreak of the epidemic in Europe, the health commissioner for the City of St. Louis was Dr. Max C. Starkloff. He studied the migration of the disease, monitoring its pace, symptoms and progress. Several East Coast cities with less restrictive measures like Boston, Philadelphia and Washington, D.C., experienced nearly double the infection and casualty rates as St. Louis.

Determined to reduce the casualties as much as possible, Starkloff instituted measures that had worked successfully elsewhere. He advised avoiding fatigue, alcohol and crowds; getting plenty of fresh air; avoiding those who are ill; and wearing masks. To obtain reliable data, physicians were required to report influenza cases.

On October 1, St. Louis had its first reported cases at Jefferson Barracks, the nation's oldest military installment west of the Mississippi. Within one week, eight hundred soldiers had been hospitalized. Barnes Hospital

St. Louis Red Cross Motor Corps on duty during 1918 influenza epidemic. *Library of Congress.*

quickly trained nurse aides and rushed them to the base, and the outbreak was contained. (By the end of the outbreak, Jefferson Barracks had two thousand cases.)

The virus meanwhile had spread to the city, and on October 7, St. Louis closed most public places – theaters, schools, bars and churches. The clergy supported the closures in order to safeguard their parishioners and advised how to worship at home. Gatherings of 20 or more were prohibited. On the eighth, the prohibition was expanded to pool halls, playgrounds, library reading rooms, fraternal lodges and the courts. Since schools were closed, the Taussig Open Air School at 1540 South Grand Boulevard was turned into an emergency hospital. Private hospitals refused to accept influenza patients, so people had to turn to public institutions, and by October 11, City Hospital on Lafayette Avenue was full. An unforeseen side effect was the number of orphaned children; in ten weeks, the flu killed 20,000 people in New York City and left 31,000 orphans.

World War I was in full swing; factories involved in war production could not simply stop. But factories of all types did institute staggered work schedules, which reduced the density of people at the workplace and on the streetcars, which also had restrictions. Health officials and civic leaders worked with the press to explain the situation and what to expect. The

American Red Cross printed over one million four-page informational pamphlets. Because of the city's diverse population, St. Louis' Red Cross had versions printed in eight languages: English, Polish, Russian, Yiddish, Hungarian, Italian, Bohemian and Spanish.

Health restrictions met with some degree of objection, primarily due to two factors: negative financial impact and civil liberty issues. The financial aspect is clear; businesses would suffer or even go out of business if customers stayed away.

By the time it was over, St. Louis reported 31,693 influenza cases and 2,883 deaths. Per capita, these figures were slightly higher than rural Missouri yet dramatically lower than major East Coast cities, ranking thirty-seventh among the forty-nine cities with populations above 100,000.

Washington, D.C., experienced some of the worst situations. People were dying at such a rate that by October 10 the city had run out of coffins, and bodies were piled up in the morgue. Baltimore and Philadelphia also had coffin shortages. D.C. commissioner Louis Brownlow stated that health officials discovered two railcars carrying 270 coffins to Pittsburgh, and the Board of Health rerouted them to D.C. Amid this flurry, the price of coffins skyrocketed, and people thought that manufacturers were extorting money at the expense of the suffering public.

Amid the outbreak, with no cure for influenza, medical providers could only try to minimize the symptoms. There were no vaccines or effective remedies. Where possible, people were placed outdoors for fresh air. Treatments of no value were often employed, such as laxatives, camphor oil, quinine (a malaria drug), salt water and snake oil. The only medical treatment that offered any genuine result was aspirin. Aspirin (acetylsalicylic acid) was invented in 1897 by Bayer, a German company. By 1914, aspirin was one of the most widely used medications in the world. In 1915, it became available without a prescription.

Bayer's patent expired in 1917, so dozens of companies began manufacturing the medication—perfectly timed with the outbreak of influenza in 1918. In 1917, St. Louis drug manufacturer Monsanto was one of the companies. In an ironic twist, salicylic acid is also a key component for high explosives. At the outbreak of World War I, the United Kingdom was a primary supplier of phenol. Once war broke out, the British cut off all trade, including that of phenol, with Germany.

In a second odd twist, phenol (carbolic acid) was also used in the manufacture of "diamond disc" phonograph records, invented by Thomas Edison. The product debuted in 1912. Not one to let a world war interrupt business, Edison built a phenol factory at Johnstown, Pennsylvania. It could produce a remarkable eleven tons a day. This quantity was far more than he needed, but the surplus could be sold to the British for high explosives at a healthy profit.

The Germans were not keen on the British obtaining an additional supply of phenol for high explosives, so they devised a plot. They set up a shell company called the Chemical Exchange Association to buy all the surplus phenol from Edison, a whopping three tons a day. This effectively prevented the phenol from being shipped to Britain for the manufacture of high explosives. In addition, it could then be used to put the New York Bayer plant back in operation. The U.S. Secret Service discovered the plot in July 1915, but not before the Germans had diverted enough phenol to make an astonishing 4.5 million pounds of high explosives. The facts were exposed in the press, and the case became known as the "Great Phenol Plot."

As a side note, the town of Sauget, Illinois (across the river from St. Louis) used to be named Monsanto, after the chemical plant there. In a final strange twist, in 2018, the German Bayer company purchased the St. Louis–based Monsanto, producer of aspirin during World War I.

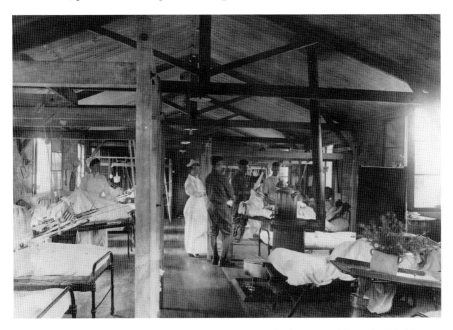

Interior view of a surgical hut showing patients and medical personnel from the Washington University School of Medicine at Base Hospital 21, Rouen, France, circa 1917. *Bernard Becker Medical Library Archives, Washington University School of Medicine.*

Turning back the hands of time, St. Louis also played a vital role in combating the influenza outbreak overseas. During World War I, in May 1917, the U.S. Army and the American Red Cross created fifty base hospitals with staff from university medical centers. In St. Louis, Washington University doctors and nurses were assigned to staff Base Hospital 21, a 1,350-bed hospital in Rouen, France. They were among the first Americans to reach the European war zone.

Base Hospital 21 treated 61,453 patients over eighteen months. With the outbreak of influenza, the staff was heavily taxed, and in October 1918, the daily number of patients reached 1,950.

Amid the horrors of war and deaths due to influenza, St. Louis fared significantly better than most cities, because it imposed such strict measures. The city recorded no more than 2,883 deaths, while Philadelphia listed more than 10,000.

And finally, as if the nation hadn't had enough, a year later, on October 28, 1919, Congress passed the Volstead Act, better known as the National Prohibition Act, and the nation went from pandemic to compulsory sobriety.

SPIRITUALISM

The Big Con

Fom levitating tables to excreting ectoplasm: in the late 1800s, a movement called spiritualism swept the nation, and St. Louis was an epicenter.

The era after the Civil War was a desperate, tumultuous time. With 680,000 dead and countless homes, businesses and farms destroyed, there was hardly a family unaffected. In this climate, opportunists preyed on people's sorrow and fear, promising the mourning survivors the hope of communicating with loved ones in the afterlife.

Spiritualists claimed to have the ability to communicate with the dead. "Mediums" put on shows that included levitating chairs, banging drums and vomiting ectoplasm as manifestations of the departed.

It reached the highest levels of society. Mary Todd Lincoln, the wife of the president of the United States, held séances in the White House in a desperate effort to speak with her deceased youngest son, William, in 1862. In Britain, Sir Arthur Conan Doyle was the world's best-known proponent. By 1900, an estimated eight million people followed spiritualism in Europe and the United States.

Two of the nation's most famous mediums were the Fox sisters, Kate and Maggie, from New York. They put on live performances, channeling the dead, who would respond with knocking that had no discernable point of origin.

Skeptics felt that spiritualism was a sham, but the movement's advocates strongly supported its practitioners. In St. Louis in 1859, the founder of the

Left: Kate and Maggie Fox, spirit mediums from Rochester, New York, during one of their visits to St. Louis, 1852. *Missouri Historical Society*.

Right: Dr. Joseph Nash McDowell. *Missouri Historical Society*.

Missouri Medical College, Joseph Nash McDowell, scientifically "proved" that the Fox sisters were not frauds.

The Fox sisters traveled to every major city, putting on séances, including in St. Louis. In January and July 1852, they gave demonstrations at the Planter's House Hotel (this was also where the National Coffee Roasters Association held meetings (see chapter "Coffee Was King"). Numerous other spiritualists lectured and put on demonstrations at St. Louis' Mercantile Library.

The endorsement of believers such as the aforementioned McDowell gave the movement credence. There was hardly a more reputable man in St. Louis. He founded the Missouri Medical College (aka McDowell's Medical College, or Gratiot College), the first medical school founded west of the Mississippi River.

The school was located at Gratiot and Ninth and Eighth Streets (see chapter "Civil War Contraband Hospitals and Black Healthcare"). It was one of two institutions that evolved into the Washington University School of Medicine.

McDowell was a firm believer and even claimed to have seen a vision of his dead mother. He was involved in séances to communicate with his dead daughter. Stories later surfaced that he engaged in grave robbing to perform autopsies. In a weird, unrelated side note, he studied at Transylvania University in Kentucky.

The stories only get stranger, and you would have to thoroughly investigate them to separate myth from truth. One story has it that McDowell preserved his daughter's body in a container filled with alcohol and suspended it in a cave in nearby Hannibal, Missouri, to retain her presence on earth.

Spiritualism continued through the end of World War I. Ultimately, skeptics debunked the many charlatans who preyed on the grief-stricken, revealing their tricks and techniques and exposing them as frauds. The famous Harry Houdini made it his mission to expose mediums. He observed their practices and then demonstrated deceptions. Flash photography was also used to capture the wires or other tricks used to fool attendees.

It is remarkable that people in the 1930s could have still believed. In 1888, Maggie Fox of the famous Fox sisters actually confessed that it was all a sham. She appeared on stage at the New York Academy of Music and publicly announced that she and Kate had made the rapping noises by cracking their toes.

Eventually, every claim, show and phenomenon was exposed, not just as untruths but also as purposeful hoaxes. People had made careers by creating clever devices to fool millions of people. Today, unbelievably, the phenomena live on through modern counterparts such as psychic hotlines and a host of other similar scams.

PLANTER'S HOUSE HOTEL, FOURTH STREET AND CHESTNUT STREET, ST. LOUIS, MISSOURI 63102

ST. LOUIS MERCANTILE LIBRARY, 1 UNIVERSITY BOULEVARD, ST. LOUIS, MISSOURI 63121

ST. LOUIS ERUV

*T*here is a twenty-mile wire infrastructure encircling a seven-square-mile area within St. Louis. It does not transmit anything—electricity or telephone or cable service—nothing at all. Most residents of St. Louis have never heard of it.

Its purpose? It is a religious symbolic boundary established by the Orthodox Jewish community called an eruv. Most cities with an appreciable Jewish population have one. In 1979, there were ten in the United States; today, there are hundreds.

According to Torah law, Jews are to refrain from work during the Sabbath. (This is a simplification of a complex topic). The Jewish Sabbath begins on Friday night at sundown, and many activities during this period are prohibited.

As in many religions, the rules are interpreted differently. More traditional views do not define "work" simply as going to a job. It can include labor or efforts such as carrying objects and using cars, electricity or even keys.

Again, like all religions, there are exceptions to the rule. The "no work" rule does not apply to lifting or carrying objects within a private area, defined as an area with set borders.

An eruv is meant to symbolically define a collective property, the Jewish community, thereby granting an exception to the rule within its boundaries. Ordinarily in large urban areas, an eruv is defined by wires on poles. But they can also consist of other boundary markers, such as fences or even

The eruv line is visible running through the woods of Stacy Park in Olivette.

railroad lines, or natural boundaries like a river. Ultimately, the marker can be included as long as it creates an uninterrupted circuit.

St. Louis' first eruv was established in 1893 (alternatively listed as 1875) and had its boundary near the St. Louis Water Works at Bissell's Point. In that era, the primary mode of transportation in the city was the electric streetcar. The eruv was marked by existing features such as telegraph wires. It enclosed what the press of the day referred to as the Jewish ghetto (the original meaning of the word).

The current University City eruv was established in 1994. Chesterfield also has one. Manhattan has one eighteen miles long made of fishing line that costs $125,000 a year to maintain. Every day, someone drives its perimeter to see that it is intact.

THREE OF THE NATION'S REMAINING SEVEN STANDPIPE WATER TOWERS

S t. Louis is home to three of the nation's last seven standpipe water towers. These massive stone towers (each at least 150 feet tall) were used during the late nineteenth and early twentieth centuries to regulate water pressure in city systems. At their peak, there were at least four hundred standpipe water towers in the United States.

They arose out of an important engineering problem: how to maintain continuous pressure in a water system with hundreds of thousands of users. In the 1870s, St. Louis' population exceeded three hundred thousand. The original system was driven by old steam-driven water pumps. An inherent flaw in the system was the significant surge in water pressure. The principle was based on an average consumption of water at any given moment. But if more people used water at one time, pressure dropped; conversely, if fewer people used it, turning on a tap would result in an explosive gusher. To alleviate the surges (which caused great shaking in the pipes), large vertical "standpipes" were created. To cloak their unappealing utilitarian purpose, cities built beautiful towers around them. Eventually, standpipe towers were replaced with elevated reservoirs, tanks or direct pressure pumping, and the brief but glorious era of the standpipe towers came to an end.

The youngest of St. Louis' towers, the Compton Hill Water Tower, was (surprisingly) active for just thirty-one years, from 1898 to 1929. This beautifully preserved Victorian structure is 179 feet tall and is made of

Above, left: Grand Avenue Water Tower (the White Tower), built 1871.

Above, right: Bissell Street Water Tower (the Red Tower), built 1886.

Right: Compton Hill Water Tower on South Grand, built 1898.

rusticated limestone, brick and terra-cotta. It was a popular destination during the 1904 World's Fair, and over five thousand visitors climbed the 198 iron stairs in the spiral staircase to get a magnificent 360-degree view of the city. The Grand Avenue Water Tower holds the record as the world's largest freestanding Corinthian column.

Grand Avenue Water Tower (the White Tower), North Twentieth Street and East Grand Boulevard, St. Louis, Missouri 63107

Bissell Street Water Tower (the Red Tower), 1423 Bissell Street, St. Louis, Missouri 63107

Compton Hill Water Tower, 1700–1898 South Grand Boulevard, St. Louis, Missouri 63104

TOASTED RAVIOLI

St. Louis is often cited as the birthplace of the ice cream cone, hamburgers, hot dogs, peanut butter, iced tea and cotton candy (thanks to the 1904 World's Fair). We can also lay claim to such dishes as the gooey butter cake, frozen custard (a concrete), pork steak, St. Louis–style pizza, the St. Louis slinger, the St. Paul Sandwich and, number one on this list, toasted ravioli.

If you have been living under a rock in St. Louis and do not know what ravioli is, it is an Italian dish of a dough pocket (circular or square) filled with meat, cheese or spinach. They are boiled and topped with oil or red or white sauce and often topped with grated cheese. The toasted version was created right here when a chef accidentally dropped some uncooked ravioli into a deep fryer—voilà, a truly delicious food was born.

But the debate about who created it continues to this day. You see, there are two claimants: Oldani's at 2132 Edwards Street (now occupied by Mama Campisi's), and Angelo's Pasta House at 5226 Shaw Avenue (now Charlie Gitto's on The Hill).

An eyewitness claiming that Oldani's invented it was Mickey Garagiola, older brother of baseball Hall of Famer Joe Garagiola. He claimed to have been present when the chef (Fritz) made the happy accident.

The root of the confusion is probably that Oldani's was owned by Lou Oldani Sr. and Angelo's was owned by his brother Angelo Oldani. Regardless, both sides stick to the claim.

Above: Mama Campisi's (Oldani's), 2020.

Right: Charlie Gitto's on The Hill (Angelo's), 2020.

The delicious dish is here and is on the menu of every Italian restaurant in St. Louis. So what does it matter?! Buon appetito!

MAMA CAMPISI'S (OLDANI'S), 2132 EDWARDS STREET, ST. LOUIS, MISSOURI 63110
CHARLIE GITTO'S ON THE HILL (ANGELO'S), 5226 SHAW AVENUE, ST. LOUIS, MISSOURI 63110

TOMB OF THE UNKNOWN SOLDIER

Identity Discovered

The grave of Air Force first lieutenant Michael Joseph Blassie was moved to Jefferson Barracks National Cemetery from the Tomb of the Unknown Soldier in Arlington National Cemetery after DNA tests confirmed his identity.

The Tomb of the Unknown Soldier is a national burial site at Arlington National Cemetery to honor the war dead whose bodies were unidentifiable. The first soldier interred was from World War I, and others have since been added for World War II, the Korean War and the Vietnam War.

On May 28, 1984, President Ronald Reagan presided over the interment of the Vietnam Unknown. As there were no known relatives, the president acted in the family's stead by accepting the Medal of Honor and the interment flag at the end of the ceremony.

Later, a woman named Jean Blassie provided evidence suggesting that the body of the Vietnam Unknown was likely that of her son, Air Force first lieutenant Michael Joseph Blassie, and she requested the remains be tested.

On May 14, 1998, the remains were exhumed. DNA tests were conducted and concluded that the remains were indeed those of Lieutenant Blassie. His body was returned to his family and reburied in Jefferson Barracks National Cemetery in his hometown of St. Louis on July 11, 1998.

The now-empty crypt has remained empty and was installed with a cover with the inscription, "Honoring and Keeping Faith with America's Missing Servicemen, 1958–1975."

JEFFERSON BARRACKS NATIONAL CEMETERY, 2900 SHERIDAN ROAD, ST. LOUIS, MISSOURI 63125

TRAINS, UNION STATION AND
THE WHISPERING ARCH

Before the advent of trains, every crate of finished goods from the East Coast was either shipped by boat and sailed up the Mississippi on steamboat or was shipped overland and floated across the river.

While the eastern half of the nation was busily building huge stretches of rail lines, visionaries realized that it would be necessary to extend those lines all the way to the West Coast. This would enable a faster and less expensive way to get goods and people to and from boomtown cities on the coast, especially California after gold was discovered there in 1848. In the early nineteenth century, the two alternatives for traveling from New York to California were overland (about 140 days by wagon) or the 18,000 nautical miles by sea around the tip of South America (about 100 days).

In 1851, shipbuilder William Webb constructed the largest and fastest sailing ship in the world, the *Challenge*. Webb offered its captain a $10,000 bonus if he could sail from New York to San Francisco in 90 days. Despite the incentive, the best he could do was 108 days.

There was no Panama Canal at the time, but in 1850, overland routes were established at the Isthmus of Panama and in Nicaragua, and a person could sail to Central America, make the short overland trip and then take a paddle-wheel steamer up the coast in as little as forty-five days. In 1849, about 67,000 settlers arrived in California (42,000 over land and 25,000 by sea). Eventually, the Panama Canal reduced time by enabling ships to sail nonstop.

A train of the Missouri Pacific Railroad crashes on its inaugural trip near Hermann, Missouri, November 1, 1855. *Missouri Historical Society.*

All this is said to illustrate the earnest effort to expedite travel to the West Coast, but the ultimate answer was to build rail lines from coast to coast. It was St. Louis' ambition to serve as the hub through which all rail traffic traveled, stimulating trade, supplying travelers, providing jobs and enabling lucrative deals.

The earliest serious plans about expanding railroads westward took place in April 1835 at the first Missouri Railroad Convention in St. Louis. In March 1849, the city secured a Missouri charter for the Pacific Railroad to extend from St. Louis to Kansas City with the ultimate objective of reaching the Pacific Ocean. A few months later, in October 1849, a National Railroad Convention was held (again in St. Louis), and Missouri senator Thomas Hart Benton (whose statue stands in Lafayette Park) delivered a speech for the development of a railroad to the Pacific coast. While a transcontinental railroad was far from a new idea, the decision of where to run such a railroad was the subject of great debate. A civil engineer named Theodore Judah, who helped build the first railroad in California, advocated a route through Nebraska, Wyoming, Utah, Nevada and California. A New Yorker named Asa Whitney urged a line north to Puget Sound.

Despite other proposals, the Pacific Railroad became the first pioneer railroad west of the Mississippi, with its charter in 1849. Construction began on July 4, 1851, and the railway began operations on a short stretch of track a year later. The first passenger train west of the Mississippi departed a station near Fourteenth Street and Chouteau Avenue at 1:00 p.m. on December 9, 1852, headed to Kirkwood, Missouri.

A few years later, the Pacific Railroad was connected to the state capitol in Jefferson City. On November 1, 1855, the inaugural trip was made with much fanfare, leaving St. Louis for the capitol with six hundred prominent passengers. A bridge collapsed, killing thirty people in the first major deadly bridge collapse in the nation's history.

The next segment, to Sedalia, 188 miles west of St. Louis, was completed in 1861. The final leg of the Pacific Railroad to Kansas City was not completed for years, until September 1865, because of disruption due to the Civil War (April 1861–April 1865), a financial crisis and cost overruns.

In March 1853, Congress passed the Army Appropriation Act, which provided for the survey of possible rail routes to the Pacific. It is quite an oddity that this was directed by the secretary of war, Jefferson Davis, who years later became the president of the Confederate States of America.

A steamboat ferry shuttling a train across the Mississippi into Carondelet near St. Louis. *Missouri Historical Society.*

The rest, as they say, is history. The Railroad Act of 1862 effectively enabled the completion of a transcontinental railroad, creating the Union Pacific Railroad. It was joined with the Central Pacific line on May 10, 1869, at Promontory, Utah.

Now a train could run all the way across the country. At least, you would think so. The oddity is that there was one break in the intercontinental railroad—at St. Louis. The Eads Bridge was not completed until five years after the last spike at Promontory.

You see, until this time, trains had been arriving from the East Coast, stopping on the Illinois bank, then loading their cars onto a ferry, which would transport them across the Mississippi. So, even though the actual rail line ran from coast to coast, it was severed, and the Wiggins Ferry made an absolute fortune shuttling cars across the river.

But with the bridge's completion on July 4, 1874, the rails were finally truly coast-to-coast lines. However, many railroad operators had not obtained permits to operate in Missouri, so they could not legally cross the bridge and enter St. Louis. The Wiggins Ferry continued to float train cars across the river, circumventing the bridge and tunnel, providing no revenues for the bridge. As such, by 1875, the Eads Bridge was bankrupt. Shortly thereafter, it was purchased at auction by the St. Louis Bridge Company for a third of the building cost.

One of the ferries that shuttled trains across the Mississippi, called transfer ferries, was the SS *Albatross*, built by the Louisiana and Mississippi Valley Transfer Company in 1907. It transported trains and railway cars between Vicksburg, Mississippi, and Delta Point, Louisiana. It was later renovated to become the SS *Admiral*, famous in St. Louis for operating as a casino in the early 1990s.

Other routes were developed and continued the process of connecting all parts of the vast nation. The effect on St. Louis was incomprehensible. Settlers en masse began migrating west, faster, more cheaply and with a much higher degree of safety. And they could arrange transport of much more than they could carry on a wagon. They settled along the railroads, and towns sprang up overnight. Businesses from hardware stores to lumber mills to general stores came with them to meet the needs of new arrivals. What these new people returned on the rails were raw materials, trade items from Pacific ports: cattle, crops and minerals, especially gold.

Rail traffic was so intense in St. Louis that a new terminal was built in 1875; it proved inadequate to accommodate all the trains in a single location, so yet another station was built. Union Station opened on September 1, 1894.

The Whispering Arch in Union Station, with beautiful stained glass and superb craftmanship, 2020.

It was built in only two years using only hand tools by skilled artisans. It went on to become one of the largest and busiest passenger rail terminals in the world. During World War II, it received an average of 150 passenger trains a day; two million solders a month passed through. As rail traffic faded out, due to the rise of the automobile and the superhighway, the once-glorious facility went dormant in 1978 and fell into decay. The only life it saw for years was a moment in the spotlight, as the Grand Hall was the setting for a scene in John Carpenter's movie *Escape from New York*. It has since been part of a rejuvenation effort, first as retail space, which eventually fizzled, but more recently with the revitalization of the surrounding area and creation of the St. Louis Aquarium, the Wheel and retail shops.

Many people know this fact, but I am surprised more do not. Inside the main entrance to the Grand Hall (on Market Street) is the "Whispering Arch." It is an architectural anomaly that allows a person on one side of the arch to speak to and be heard by a person on the other side. Above the arch you will see some splendid stained glass. The accompanying photo is of the top of the arch from the second floor.

Just as the horse and buggy were replaced by the streetcar and train, so too, over time, were they replaced with the automobile, highways and the airplane. We often wax nostalgic about the loss of the romantic parts of previous eras such as the streetcar and the Pony Express, but the reality is that they were simply part of life for a sliver of time until inefficiency or cost rendered them unsustainable.

GRAND HALL OF UNION STATION, 1820 MARKET STREET, ST. LOUIS, MISSOURI 63103

TWELFTH-CENTURY ENGLISH CHAPEL DISMANTLED AND SHIPPED HERE

*O*n more than one occasion, the *St. Louis Post-Dispatch* and the *Riverfront Times* awarded the title "No. 1 Fried Chicken in St. Louis" to a restaurant that was is not in St. Louis. In fact, it was not even in Missouri. Gallagher's in Waterloo, Illinois, is only a thirty-minute drive from downtown. It was included because we in St. Louis have a pretty fluid idèa of the "Greater Metropolitan St. Louis Area," understanding that the City of St. Louis is actually pretty small and has around three hundred thousand of the almost three million people in the metro area. That is why this story of "St. Louis" history is placed at Westminster College in Fulton, Missouri, over an hour's drive west of the suburbs.

The original Church of St. Mary the Virgin, Aldermanbury, was built in London early in the twelfth century, and sadly it was destroyed in 1666 during the Great Fire of London. In 1677, the chapel was restored using some of the original medieval stone. The new chapel was designed by the same architect who designed St. Paul's Cathedral in London.

The church was burned down a second time on December 29, 1940, right before Christmas, by German bombers during World War II. Only the outer walls, columns and bell tower survived. The church remained in ruins until 1960, when members of the St. Louis chapter of the English-Speaking Union suggested building a memorial to Winston Churchill on the campus of Westminster College in Fulton. British and Americans donated $1.5 million to move the church.

Church of St. Mary the Virgin, Aldermanbury, with a statue of Winston Churchill outside, 2020. All seven thousand stones were brought from England and the structure was reassembled exactly as it stood, one block from the home of William Shakespeare. This sculpture by Don Wiegand and Richard J. Mahoney stands outside the church.

In 1965, each of the seven thousand stones (weighing a total of 650 tons) was cleaned, labeled and packed, with notes about the location of each stone. They were shipped to Virginia and then shipped by train to Fulton. There is little detail of how, but somehow in transit, the stones or notes were confused, and those charged with rebuilding the chapel had a terrible time figuring out where everything went. It was a bit of a Humpty Dumpty situation.

Once the exterior was completed, it took another two years to duplicate the interior—the organ, stained glass, pulpit, baptismal font and balcony. Everything was carefully reproduced. Five bronze bells for the tower were created by a Dutch firm. (Interesting side notes about the chapel's history are that William Shakespeare lived a block away, and John Milton's second wife was a member of the church.)

In March 1946, Churchill delivered one of the most famous and important speeches of the twentieth century in this church, the "Sinews of

Peace" speech (better known as the "Iron Curtain" speech). At end of World War II, our Soviet allies did not share our interest in restoring the former countries they had "liberated." They instead took the opportunity to install communist governments rather than restore the previous governments.

The heart of Churchill's speech was that the Soviets were initiating a political takeover, with an "iron curtain" dividing Eastern and Western Europe. The speech set the tone of the Cold War, with the Soviets supporting communist incursions and the United States countering (notably in Cuba, Korea and Vietnam). After hearing the speech, Stalin denounced it as "war mongering" and stated that Churchill's comments about the "English-speaking world" were imperialist racism.

After the Berlin Wall was taken down, a large section was brought to the Churchill Museum at Westminster College in Fulton. The thirty-two-foot-long, eleven-foot-tall wall was originally near the Brandenburg Gate.

Westminster College, West Seventh Street, Fulton, Missouri 65251

UNDERGROUND
COLD WAR BUNKER

The St. Louis Civil Defense Control Center

D uring the Cold War, there was an ever-present threat of nuclear attack. It was mortifying to watch the "Duck and Cover" cartoon about Bert the Turtle responding to a nuclear detonation. Schoolchildren practiced hiding under their desks when they heard air raid sirens or saw the blast. In reality, if you saw the blast, crawling under your desk would be like putting a paper bag over your head. It gave parents an illusory hope that nuclear war was somehow survivable.

In preparation for the "Big One," one of the government's top priorities was to safeguard elected officials and communications so the government

Interior view of the civil defense shelter. *St. Louis County Police Department's Office of Emergency Management.*

could still function. In 1962, the federal government spent $14 million building a massive, secret underground nuclear bomb shelter at the posh Greenbrier Resort in West Virginia with concrete walls three feet thick for members of the U.S. Congress. It had beds, food, medical care, fuel reserves, communications, water and an air-filtration system for 1,100 people for six months. It was kept secret for thirty years.

Keeping with the times, St. Louis County built its own "bomb shelter lite" version of the Greenbrier, hidden two stories underground in Chesterfield. Yes, we had our own nuclear fallout shelter for the mayor of St. Louis, the county executive and seventy other officials and their families. It had all the same essential supplies and services to sustain the inhabitants for two weeks.

After the Cold War largely cooled, the facility was relegated to less ominous catastrophes. Its communications facilities have been used to manage responses to floods and other natural disasters.

14847 LADUE BLUFFS CROSSING DRIVE, CHESTERFIELD, MISSOURI 63017

U.S. ARMY RETALIATORY EXECUTION OF POWS

Since before the Hague Conventions of 1899 or the Geneva Conventions in 1929, the United States has maintained a rule of civility toward prisoners of war. For the most part. But this is a story of how six POWs were randomly selected by the U.S. Army to be executed in St. Louis, not for any crime they had committed, but out of revenge.

The American Civil War was a very fluid and messy affair. Official accounts show maps with neatly drawn lines shaded in blue and gray. That is far from reality. While Missouri was officially a Union state, many citizens either left the state and joined the Confederacy or were Southern sympathizers. Some even carried out their own active war against the Union behind the front lines.

Allegiances varied from town to town, even within families; it is often cited that this was a war of brother against brother. Civilians on both sides took every opportunity to burn, loot and destroy property of the opposition, even disguising themselves in the uniforms of their enemy to infiltrate. The official battle lines bore no reality during the ongoing guerrilla warfare among much of the population in border states.

The official government death tally excludes deaths in the civilian guerrilla war—the "war within a war"—which amounted to as many as 3 percent of Missouri's population (twenty-seven thousand).

A large group of Missouri rebel guerrillas had been carrying out raids near Doniphan, led by Colonel Timothy Reeves. Seeking to put an end to

Gratiot Street Prison, a former medical college at Eighth and Gratiot Streets in St. Louis that the Union turned into a prison to house rebel prisoners of war and civilian sympathizers. Six Confederates were executed on October 29, 1864. *Missouri Historical Society.*

the incursions, Union major general James H. Wilson led his troops on a surprise raid of the rebel camp on Christmas Day 1863. During the raid, the Union troops killed thirty-five guerrillas and freed one hundred of their captives. Reeves escaped. Nine months later, Wilson himself was captured by Confederate troops, and Confederate general Sterling Price (a former Missouri governor) turned Wilson over to Reeves. A month later, Reeves had Wilson and six Union soldiers killed southwest of Washington, Missouri.

The Union commander in Missouri, Major General William Rosecrans, was outraged by the murders. In an act of revenge, he ordered that six Confederate prisoners of war be selected at random and executed. The six POWs were chosen from St. Louis' Gratiot Street Prison (for Confederate soldiers and sympathizers) at Eighth and Gratiot Streets in St. Louis (just east of where Purina is today). On October 29, 1864, they were taken by covered wagon about two miles south to a field northeast of present-day Jefferson and Shenandoah.

About three thousand people, most of them Union soldiers, came to watch. The prisoners were tied to poles and blindfolded. One of the POWs, a twenty-two-year-old named Charles W. Minniken, asked to speak: "I am now to be shot for what other men have done." A firing squad of thirty-six soldiers then shot the innocent prisoners. Their bodies were found in Franklin County and later relocated to Jefferson Barracks National Cemetery. The cemetery is for American servicemen and women and their families, and the graves of the six men are in a section among other Confederate soldiers.

EIGHTH AND GRATIOT STREETS, ST. LOUIS, MISSOURI 63103 (NOW PART OF
THE PURINA CAMPUS)

THE WAY OUT OF DARKNESS

The First School to Teach Braille

*I*n the 1900s, the scientific era gave birth to many movements across the world for the expansion of knowledge and the betterment of man. One offshoot of this thinking was the eugenics movement, which followed the thoughts of Darwin that inheritance is a factor in human evolution and that traits—both good and bad—are passed along from parent to child. Therefore, positive traits can be enhanced (such as in breeding stronger horses). This saw its most emphatic champion in the German eugenics program. Negative traits, carried through "germplasma," could be "bred out" of a species.

This thinking was seeded in Missouri by Harry H. Laughlin, who graduated from what is now Truman State University in Kirksville, Missouri, roughly two hundred miles northwest of St. Louis. He wrote extensively about genetic inheritance, believing that traits such as shiftlessness, feeblemindedness, tendency toward vagrancy and crime and promiscuousness were inherited. If your father had committed a crime, you likely inherited his propensity for crime—the apple doesn't fall far from the tree. Laughlin's proposed solution was for the sterilization of "undesirables." In 1922, he published an article on American sterilization policy, "Eugenical Sterilization in the United States," which addressed (in terms of the era) the feebleminded, the insane, criminals, epileptics, alcoholics, blind people, deaf people, people with deformities and indigent people.

By 1914, twelve states had passed sterilization laws, beginning with Indiana in 1907. In 1922, Laughlin drafted a template to assist states in

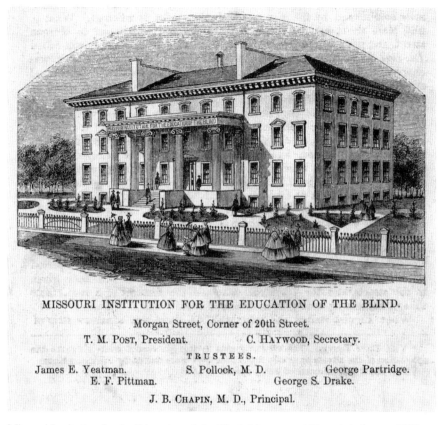

MISSOURI INSTITUTION FOR THE EDUCATION OF THE BLIND.

Morgan Street, Corner of 20th Street.

T. M. POST, President.   C. HAYWOOD, Secretary.

TRUSTEES.

James E. Yeatman.   S. Pollock, M. D.   George Partridge.
E. F. Pittman.   George S. Drake.

J. B. CHAPIN, M. D., Principal.

Missouri Institution for the Education of the Blind, Morgan and Twentieth Streets, 1860. *Missouri Historical Society.*

implementing these laws. At the height of the movement, thirty states forced more than sixty thousand sterilizations of disabled individuals alone. Missouri had several bills put forward for compulsory sterilization.

In 1927, the topic gained national attention with the case of a seventeen-year-old patient at the Virginia State Colony for Epileptics and Feeble Minded, Carrie Buck. She had been raped by her stepfather and had given birth to a child out of wedlock, which was covered up by the foster parents. Her biological mother, Emma, had been institutionalized at the Virginia State Colony a few years earlier. It was the presumption, therefore, that the newborn child, Vivian Elaine, was destined to join the ranks of her mother and grandmother and become a ward of the state, at taxpayer expense. Supreme Court justice Oliver Wendell Holmes Jr. wrote of the case, "Three generations of imbeciles is enough."

The U.S. Supreme Court ruled that compulsory sterilization of certain groups, such as people with mental impairment, could be considered in the public good and was therefore permissible. Now you know how it must have felt to live in a country where the highest court in the land allowed the government to sterilize a citizen because of something their ancestor did, because they could not read or because they were born with an impairment. That said, Missouri did not enact a law allowing compulsory sterilization.

St. Louis, in contrast, espoused the view that the inability to see, whether from birth or through the loss of sight, was a physical impairment, much like the loss of a limb, and that it did not affect the person. With proper training, the individual could develop just like all others. In 1851, St. Louis became the first city in the Western Hemisphere to teach the reading and writing of Braille, at the Missouri School for the Blind (officially named Missouri Institution for the Education of the Blind) on Magnolia Avenue.

The concept that blindness was simply a condition rather than an overarching human defect originated in France in 1784. After viewing blind men in a café in Paris wearing dunce caps and playing musical instruments badly to amuse patrons, Valentin Haüy founded the first school for the blind. He created a system to make books for the blind using print type with Roman lettering, cast in reverse and pressed in from the opposing side. This in effect made a printed book with raised letters instead of inked letters.

In 1824, an improved system of reading for the blind was created by a Frenchman named Louis Braille, who was himself blind. While a student at the National Institute for Blind Children in France, he developed a system using raised dots on paper. The concept of using dots rather than letters originated with another Frenchman, Charles Barbier, who served in Napoleon Bonaparte's army. Barbier created a written communication system called "night writing" so that soldiers could communicate safely at night. During wartime, it was dangerous to read messages at night by lamps, which drew gunfire and artillery. Barbier's coding method of raised dots could be read by fingertips and represented phonetic sounds.

WHISKEY MILKING SCANDAL

*T*en years before Prohibition, the State of Tennessee declared alcohol illegal, so Lem Motlow, nephew of Jack Daniel, moved some of the family distillery to St. Louis (4000 Duncan Avenue, presently the west side of IKEA).

It was business as usual for ten years. Then, in 1920, nationwide Prohibition was enacted. Jack Daniel could not distill whiskey, nor was the company allowed to sell the nine hundred barrels of whiskey already produced on the site.

The only legal sales were for medicinal purposes, which required a doctor's prescription. (One can imagine a considerable increase in toothaches during this period). To prevent illegal distilling and sales, the warehouse was guarded by federal inspectors.

Soon, local gangs developed a system by which they could drive trucks into the alley, syphon off whiskey and replace it with a mixture of water and whiskey. In August 1923, they stole thirty-one thousand gallons. Initially, inspectors probably just jiggled the barrels to see if they were full. But eventually an inspector did a taste test and discovered the diluted mixture.

The Feds swooped in and found that only one barrel of whiskey remained. Most certainly it was an inside job, and suspicion fell on the chief guard, William Kinney, who was connected to the Egan's Rats gang. Federal agents investigated what became known as the "Whiskey Milking Scandal," and two years later, twenty-three men were convicted in the theft, including eleven prominent St. Louisans.

Jack Daniel Distilling Company building, location of the famed Whiskey Milking Scandal, 1900. *Missouri Historical Society.*

On January 4, 1926, the convicted men were brought to Track 7 at Union Station to meet a train from Indianapolis for a two-hour layover. More than four thousand people met the train to applaud the convicts of St. Louis' most notorious Prohibition-era scandal. After receiving this celebrity treatment, they were shipped off to the federal prison in Leavenworth, Kansas, aboard the train dubbed the "Leavenworth Special."

4000 DUNCAN AVENUE, ST. LOUIS, MISSOURI (NOW A SIDE ALLEY TO IKEA)

WORLD'S FIRST SKYSCRAPER

The Wainwright Building

*T*he City of St. Louis claims to be home to the world's first skyscraper, the ten-story Wainwright Building (which still stands today) at 709 Chestnut Street. It was built in 1891 by local financier and brewer Ellis Wainwright. It is the first skyscraper "in spirit."

Wainwright Building, 1907. *Missouri Historical Society*.

What does "in spirit" mean? The Wainwright Building either is the first skyscraper, or it is not. The actual title is first *skyscraper*. There were already taller buildings in both Chicago and New York before the Wainwright, but it is argued that they were not skyscrapers.

Earlier tall buildings, one apt analogy goes, were like a multitiered wedding cake, with new levels of increasingly smaller size stacked one on another. The Wainwright is a clean, solid structure with floors of equal size due to the innovation of new skeleton frame building methods conceived by Dankmar Adler and Louis Sullivan.

The Wainwright Building appears in the National Register of Historic Places, cited as "a highly influential prototype of the modern office building."

So, while New York, Chicago and St. Louis may argue the point, most architectural historians concede that the Wainwright can be considered the first true skyscraper, in spirit.

WAINWRIGHT BUILDING, 709 CHESTNUT STREET, ST. LOUIS, MISSOURI 63101

WORLD'S LARGEST AMMO PLANT AND WORLD WAR II

*T*here is surprisingly little in St. Louis to remind us of the city's role in World War II, this despite the fact that a large percentage of young men left the area, women took jobs once relegated to men, rationing was instituted, consumer spending was affected and, at the height of the war, more than 75 percent of the city's manufacturers had retooled for war production.

Factories that produced locomotive wheels were converted to the production of tank parts, hardware factories made airplane rivets and coffin manufacturers produced ribs for gliders. St. Louis was home to the world's largest production plant of small arms ammunition, the St. Louis Ordnance Plant, at Goodfellow and Bircher. This was a government-owned, contractor-operated facility that at its peak employed thirty-five thousand people twenty-four hours a day, seven days a week. It produced 250 million cartridges a month. During the war, noted attorney and conservative activist Phyllis Schlafly worked the night shift test-firing rifles and machine guns while attending Washington University.

On the home front, American housewives collected fats for the production of explosives. The American Fat Salvage Committee was formed to encourage the collection of fats for the war effort. It was not a popular program, as fats from bacon and red meats were used in cooking. Propaganda films informed reluctant housewives that every year Americans threw away two billion pounds of household fats, with enough glycerin for ten billion artillery shells.

The Curtis-Wright factory. *Missouri Historical Society*.

St. Louis was home to several aircraft manufacturers, all of which were engaged in war production. Factories for McDonnell Aircraft Corporation and Curtiss-Wright Corporation at Lambert Field produced more than three thousand military aircraft during this period. Curtiss-Wright built the P-40 fighter, McDonnell Aircraft Company built the C-47 cargo aircraft and Robertson Aircraft Corporation built the WACO CG4 glider.

The GM/Chevrolet plant produced the invaluable six-wheel-drive amphibious vehicle, the DUKW, and Monsanto converted entirely to war production, producing chemicals used in the making of TNT, chlorine gas and sulfa compounds that treated infections. Emerson Electric in Ferguson assembled turrets for B-24 bombers. The American Car and Foundry Company's St. Louis plant produced over one million fuses a month for the army and navy, as well as eight thousand carburetors a day. Its St. Charles plant produced 1,500 M3 light tanks plus components such as hull plates for drydocks and LST boat sections.

Robertson Aircraft factory workers grinding engine valves between the wars, March 23, 1928. *Missouri Historical Society*.

St. Louis holds the unpleasant distinction of being home to the nation's first U.S. military officer to be convicted of treason. During the war, Lieutenant Martin James Monti defected to Germany and was later convicted of desertion, theft and twenty-one acts of treason.

St. Louis Ordnance Plant, 4300/4800 Goodfellow Boulevard, Saint Louis, Missouri 63120

BIBLIOGRAPHY

Abbott, Karen. "The Fox Sisters and the Rap on Spiritualism." *Smithsonian Magazine*, October 30, 2012. https://www.smithsonianmag.com.
———. "The 1904 Olympic Marathon May Have Been the Strangest Ever." *Smithsonian Magazine*, August 7, 2012. https://www.smithsonianmag.com.
About St. Louis. "World War II and St. Louis." https://aboutstlouis.com.
Alexander, Kathy. "The Chouteaus—Early Traders." Legends of America. Updated January 2022. https://www.legendsofamerica.com.
Allen, Michael R. "The Harnessed Channel: How the River Des Peres Became a Sewer." Preservation Research Office. November 27, 2010, http://preservationresearch.com.
American Battlefield Trust. "The Sultana Disaster." https://www.battlefields.org.
America's National Churchill Museum. "The Phoenix Continues to Rise." https://www.nationalchurchillmuseum.org.
Baldes, Bob. "The Miracle of the Shrine of St. Joseph in St. Louis." *Catholic Messenger*. http://www.catholicmessenger.net.
Bass, Laurence. "The Three Lives of Josephine Baker—Part One: Freda." Adventure in Black. March 9, 2022. https://www.adventureinblack.com.
Blaine, James G., et al. "Ought the Negro to Be Disfranchised? Ought He Have Been Enfranchised?" *North American Review*, March 1879. https://www.jstor.org/stable/25100732.
Blakemore, Erin. "Largest U.S. Hooverville Had Its Own Mayor and a Church Made of Orange Crates." History.com, June 8, 2018. https://www.history.com.
Brenc, Willie. "First Baptist Church, St. Louis, Missouri (1817–)." BlackPast.org, June 11, 2014. https://www.blackpast.org.
Brooks, Patricia. "Toasted Ravioli, the Secret of St. Louis." *New York Times*, February 25, 1987.
"Brown Shoe Company Inc." Encyclopedia.com. https://www.encyclopedia.com.

Build St. Louis. "Wondrous Anachronisms: The Standpipes and Water Intakes of the St. Louis Water System." https://www.builtstlouis.net.

Campbell House Museum. "A Thanksgiving Story: Father Dunne's Boys and Hugh Campbell." November 27, 2013. http://www.campbellhousemuseum.org.

CBS News. "Secret Cold War Tests in St. Louis Cause Worry." October 3, 2012. https://www.cbsnews.com.

Chabad on Campus. Rohr Center for Jewish Life. "St. Louis Community Eruv." http://www.stleruv.org.

City of St. Louis. "On the Map: Lynch's Slave Pens." June 15, 2018. https://www.stlouis-mo.gov.

———. "A Preservation Plan for St. Louis: Part I: Historic Contexts." https://www.stlouis-mo.gov/government/departments/planning/cultural-resources/preservation-plan/Part-I-Education.cfm.

———. "Revolutionary War Cannons: Overview for Revolutionary War Cannons in Lafayette Park." https://www.stlouis-mo.gov/parks/parks/browse-parks/amenity.cfm?id=87.

Collins, Cameron. "Hop Alley & White Lightning." *Distilled History*, July 15, 2013. https://www.distilledhistory.com/hopalley.

———. "Kingshighway's Way: A History of a St. Louis Street." NextSTL.com. February 6, 2015. https://nextstl.com.

———. "The St. Louis Motordrome." Distilled History. September 10, 2012. https://www.distilledhistory.com.

Cooper, Nathan. "Lincoln's Avoided Duel." Abraham Lincoln Presidential Library and Museum. August 19, 2021. https://presidentlincoln.illinois.gov.

Cooperman, Jeannette. "Take Care, and Don't Take the Cholera." *St. Louis Magazine*, June 26, 2010. https://www.stlmag.com.

Dixon Object Analysis. "Solving the Service Dilemma: The History of Automation in Grocery Stores." https://dixonobjectanalysis.weebly.com.

Durst, Dennis L. "The Reverend John Berry Meachum (1789–1854) of St. Louis: Prophet and Entrepreneurial Black Educator in Historiographical Perspective." *The North Star* 7, no. 2 (2004). https://www.princeton.edu/~jweisenf/northstar/volume7/durst.html.

Equal Justice Initiative. "On This Day—July 3, 1917: White Mob Terrorizes Black Residents in East. St. Louis Riots." https://calendar.eji.org/racial-injustice/jul/3.

Escape to the Silent Cities. "Girl in the Shadow Box." August 4, 2010. http://escapetothesilentcities.blogspot.com.

Everding, Gerry. "Eclipse Chasers and New Planet Tracers." *Washington Magazine* (Washington University in St. Louis), August 16, 2017. https://source.wustl.edu/2017/08/eclipse-chasers-new-planet-tracers.

Explore St. Louis. "Cherokee Street." https://explorestlouis.com.

———. "Route 66." https://explorestlouis.com.

Felten, Eric. "St. Louis—Party Central." *Wall Street Journal*, October 6, 2007.

Forest Park Highlands. "Chain of Rocks Park." https://unseenstlouis.substack.com/p/a-bridge-a-park-a-canal-chain-of.

Friedman, Carla. "May 17 1849: The St. Louis Great Fire." World History Project. https://worldhistoryproject.org.

"The Frost Campus: Name Origins and Changes." *University News* (Saint Louis University), April 27, 2017. https://unewsonline.com.

Garrison, Chad. "The True Story of the St. Louis House That Inspired *The Exorcist.*" *Riverfront Times*, October 26, 2005. https://www.riverfronttimes.com.

The Gaslight Theater. "History." http://www.gaslighttheater.net.

Gonzales, Daniel. "At Kinloch Field, Theodore Roosevelt Became the First U.S. President to Travel by Plane." *St. Louis Magazine*, January 2, 2018. https://www.stlmag.com.

Gorse, Sabrina. "The Winding Down of World War II and the St. Louis Ordnance Plant." Missouri Historical Society. March 23, 2021. https://mohistory.org/blog/ordnance-plant.

Greenwalt, Phil. "Battle of Fort San Carlos—Westernmost Battle of the American Revolution." Emerging Revolutionary War Era. May 31, 2019. https://emergingrevolutionarywar.org.

Grimm, Lisa. "St. Louis Beer History: Underground Beginnings." WeirdBeerGirl.com. March 30, 2021. https://www.lisagrimm.com.

Groceteria. "St. Louis Chain Grocery/Supermarket Locations, 1933–1975." June 20, 2019. https://www.groceteria.com.

Hawley, David. "The American Fur Company." Missouri Explorer. April 29, 2015. http://www.moexplorer.com.

Historical Marker Database. "Creve Coeur Lake Memorial Park—Water Trail." https://www.hmdb.org.

———. "Site of Daniel Boone's Cabin, 1799." https://www.hmdb.org.

Hoagland, H.E. "Early Transportation on the Mississippi." *Journal of Political Economy* 19, no. 2 (February 1911).

Holleman, Joe. "Grand Center, Home to Theaters and First Drive-Thru." *St. Louis Post-Dispatch*, May 30, 2015.

———. "Spotlight: Wide Alley Remains as Last Sign of Clay-Mine Train." *St. Louis Post-Dispatch*, June 20, 2015.

———. "Tree, Not Corpse, Tied to Tower Grove Park Headstone." *St. Louis Post-Dispatch*, December 4, 2016.

Hong, Kevin. "Maple+Pine: American Bowling Comes of Age." Vintagebowling.net. http://www.vintagebowling.net.

Influenza Encyclopedia. "St. Louis, Missouri." University of Michigan Center for the History of Medicine and Michigan Publishing. https://www.influenzaarchive.org.

Joiner, Robert. "St. Louis Struggles with Its Promise to Care for the Poor." St. Louis Public Radio. October 14, 2010. https://news.stlpublicradio.org.

Jones, Mike. "1849: We Got This—The St. Louis Cholera Epidemic." Lafayette Square. March 29, 2020. https://lafayettesquare.org.

Kahn, Eve M. "Noguchi Ceiling From 1940s Is Uncovered at U-Haul in St. Louis." *New York Times*, May 3, 2016.

Kavanaugh, Maureen. "Washington Avenue—Downtown St. Louis, MO." *Garment District*®. https://www.builtforfashion.com.

Keenoy, Ruth D. "Shoe Industry of St. Louis: 1870–1980." Next NGA West North St. Louis. December 14, 2016. https://www.stlouis-mo.gov/government/departments/sldc/project-connect/nga/history/upload/The-Shoe-Industry-of-St-Louis.pdf.

King, Gilbert. "Where the Buffalo No Longer Roamed." *Smithsonian Magazine*, July 17, 2012.

Klein, Emily. "Why Are There Foxes on the Corners of Anheuser-Busch's Brewery Building?" *St. Louis Magazine*, January 12, 2018. https://www.stlmag.com.

Klose, Roland. "The Naked Truth." March 8, 2014. https://rwklose.com.

KSDK. "One Last Look Inside Chesterfield Doomsday Shelter." April 11, 2014. www.ksdk.com.

Lee, Patrick. "Service Stations." *Los Angeles Times*, August 14, 1989.

Leonard, Mary Delach. "The Big Bird Cage: Where The Saint Louis Zoo Took Flight after the 1904 World's Fair." *St. Louis Public Radio*. May 26, 2014. https://news.stlpublicradio.org.

Lingham, Claire, and Helen Rolfe. "Delano's Dealings: The Opium Trade and the Making of a Presidential Legacy." Linda Lear Center Digital Collections and Exhibitions. https://lc-digital.conncoll.edu/exhibits/show/gold-journal/essays/delano.

The Living New Deal. "Soldiers' Memorial Building Sculptures—St. Louis MO." https://livingnewdeal.org.

"The Long Distance Balloon Races from St. Louis." *Scientific American* 97, no. 18 (November 1907): 308–9. https://www.scientificamerican.com.

"Looking at the History of Streetcars in St. Louis." *St. Louis Post-Dispatch*, May 20, 2021.

Mann, Howard. "Sorrowful Revenge by Firing Squad! True Tales of the Tenth Kansas Infantry." Civil War St. Louis. https://www.civilwarstlouis.com.

Masson, Pauline. "Missouri Mules Sent to Front Lines in WWI." eMissourian. com. January 19, 2017. https://www.emissourian.com.

McKinsey, David S. MD, et al. "The 1918 Influenza in Missouri: Centennial Remembrance of the Crisis." *Missouri Medicine* 115, no. 4 (July–August 2018): 319–24. https://www.ncbi.nlm.nih.gov/pmc/articles/PMC6140242.

Missouri History Museum. "The Civil War in Missouri: Camp Jackson." http://www.civilwarmo.org.

———. "James B. Eads." http://www.civilwarmo.org.

Missouri Pacific Historical Society. "MoPac's First 125 Years." https://www.mopac.org.

Missouri State Archives. "The Lewis & Clark Expedition." https://www.sos.mo.gov/archives/resources/lewisclark.asp.

Moody, Cassidy. "Moon Trees and Space Gums." Missouri Botanical Garden. July 19, 2019. https://discoverandshare.org/2019/07/19/moon-trees-and-space-gums.

Mound City on the Mississippi: A St. Louis History. "Cable Street Railways Introduced." City of St. Louis. https://dynamic.stlouis-mo.gov.

National Centers for Environmental Information. "On This Day: The Great St. Louis Tornado of 1896." National Oceanic and Atmospheric Administration. May 27, 2017. https://www.ncei.noaa.gov.

National Park Service. "The Dred Scott Case." https://www.nps.gov.

———. "Pony Express National Historic Trail." https://www.nps.gov.

———. "River of History—Chapter 3: Discovery and Dispossession." https://www.nps.gov.

National Today. "History of Josephine Baker." https://nationaltoday.com.

Neely, Jeremy. "'A Most Cruel and Unjust War:' The Guerrilla Struggle along the Missouri-Kansas Border." Civil War on the Western Border. Kansas City Public Library. https://civilwaronthewesternborder.org.

Newcombe, Emma. "The Legacy of the St. Louis Municipal Pool Race Riots." Governing.com. August 15, 2021. https://www.governing.com.

New Madrid, Missouri. "Strange Happenings during the Earthquakes." http://www.new-madrid.mo.us.

Newmark, Jill. "Contraband Hospital, 1862–1863: Health Care for the First Freedpeople." BlackPast.org. March 28, 2012. https://www.blackpast.org.

New York State Division of Criminal Justice Services. "The Henry System in America." Origins of the New York State Bureau of Identification. 1996. https://www.criminaljustice.ny.gov/ojis/history/henry_am.htm.

O'Neil, Tim. "April 24, 1953: 'This Is a Stickup. Everyone Stand Still!' The Southwest Bank Robbery." *St. Louis Post-Dispatch*, April 24, 2021.

———. "A Look Back: Jack Daniel's Distillery in St. Louis Was Target of Crime during Prohibition." *St. Louis Post-Dispatch*, December 8, 2021.

———. "Nov. 18 1939: The Day 'Black Tuesday' Rolled into St. Louis." *St. Louis Post-Dispatch*, November 28, 2021.

———. "St. Louis Drank the Brewers Dry: Celebrating the End of Prohibition in 1933." *St. Louis Post-Dispatch*, April 7, 2022.

Our St. Louis History, "Bridge Over Trouble Water: The Eads Bridge." 2017. www.ourstlouishistory.com.

———. "Our Native American History: St. Louis Mounds." https://www.ourstlouishistory.com.

Pearlman, Robert. "Boeing Recognized for Mercury Spacecraft by Institute of Electrical & Electronics Engineers." CollectSpace. March 2, 2021. http://www.collectspace.com.

Pfeiffer, David. "'Tony's Lab': Germ Warfare in WWI Used on Horses in the U.S." *Prologue Magazine* (National Archives) 49, no. 3 (Fall 2017). https://www.archives.gov/publications/prologue.

Price, Michael. "Missouri Horses and Mules." Missouri Over There. https://missourioverthere.org.

"Recalling the Fatal Train Wreck of 1855." *Hermann (MO) Advertiser-Courier*, May 19, 2020.

Ritter, Luke. "Anatomy, Grave-Robbing, and Spiritualism in Antebellum St. Louis." *The Confluence* (Spring/Summer 2012). https://digitalcommons.lindenwood.edu/confluence_2009/vol3/iss2/4.

Romanski, Fred J. "The Fast Mail: A History of the U.S. Railway Mail Service." *Prologue Magazine* (National Archives) 37, no. 3 (Fall 2005). https://www.archives.gov/publications/prologue.

Scharf, John Thomas. "Insurance, Telegraph, Postal Service, Gas, and Hotels." *History of Saint Louis City and County: From the Earliest Periods to Present Day* (Philadelphia, PA: Louis H. Everts, 1883). Volume 2, 1427.

Schremp Hahn, Valerie. "1904 World's Fair Plate Tells the Story of a President, a Cabin and a Coffee Company." *St. Louis Post-Dispatch*, May 19, 2017.

Schwarz, Joe. "The Great Phenol Plot. (Chemfusion)." The Free Library. https://www.thefreelibrary.com/The+great+phenol+plot.+(Chemfusion).-a080503675.

Shapka, Lindsay. "Why Do Nice Hotels Put Chocolates on Your Pillow?" *The Anthrotorian*. https://theanthrotorian.com.

Sherry, Mike. "The Gene: A Brief History of Eugenics in the Heartland: Kansas and Missouri Played Roles in Sterilization Movement." Flatland. https://flatlandkc.org.

Soulard Market. "Soulard Farmers Market St. Louis." www.soulardmarketstl.com.

Stiles, Nancy. "Phylloxera: How Missouri Saved the French Wine Industry." *Feast Magazine*, April 28, 2017. https://www.feastmagazine.com.

St. Louis Carousel. "History." https://stlouiscarousel.com.

St. Louis County, Missouri. "Creve Coeur Park. Park History." https://www.stlouiscountymo.gov/st-louis-county-departments/parks/about/park-history-documents/creve-coeur-history.

St. Louis on the Air. "St. Louis Children during the Late 1800s, Early 1900s Lived Tough Lives." St. Louis Public Radio. July 3, 2018. https://news.stlpublicradio.org.

St. Louis Post-Dispatch. "Parr Show Acts at Crystal Palace." April 18, 1961.

St. Louis Sage. "Was the Wainwright Building the First Skyscraper?" *St. Louis Magazine*, July 20, 2017. https://www.stlmag.com.

———. "What Happened to St. Louis' Pneumatic-Tube Mail System?" *St. Louis Magazine*, November 8, 2021. https://www.stlmag.com.

St. Louis Zoo. "1904 World's Fair Flight Cage and Edward K. Love Conservation Foundation Cypress Swamp." https://www.stlzoo.org.

Terminal Railroad Association of St. Louis. "TRRA History." https://www.terminalrailroad.com.

This Day in Aviation. "3 November 1926." https://www.thisdayinaviation.com.

Thomas, Bill. "Last Soldier Buried in Tomb of the Unknowns Wasn't Unknown." *Washington Post*, November 8, 2012.

Tower Grove Park. "The Ruins." https://www.towergrovepark.org.

United States Senate. "The Caning of Senator Charles Sumner. May 22, 1856." https://www.senate.gov.

Urban Review St. Louis. "St. Louis' Beer Garden History Goes Back 189 Years, Continues Today." July 10, 2012. https://www.urbanreviewstl.com.

Waymarking.com. "The Plank Road." https://www.waymarking.com.

Wikipedia. "SS Admiral (1907)." https://en.wikipedia.org.

Worrall, Simon. "Clipper Ship Owners Made Millions. Others Paid the Price." *National Geographic*, August 31, 2018. https://www.nationalgeographic.com.

Wunsch, James. "The Social Evil Ordinance." *American Heritage* 33, no. 3 (February/March 1982).

Yoma, Yulius. "History Hour: First Parachute Jump." *Aerotime Hub.* https://www.aerotime.aero/articles/17445-history-hour-first-parachute-jump.

Zielinski, Sarah. "The Tragic Tale of the Pygmy in the Zoo." *Smithsonian Magazine*, December 2, 2008. https://www.smithsonianmag.com.

ABOUT THE AUTHOR

Photo courtesy of Tim Parker Photography.

A historian and writer, Mark Zeman received his master of arts in English from California State University, Sacramento, with studies in medieval history at the University of Wales in Swansea, Great Britain. Within several disciplines, he has been a professional writer for over thirty years and has received numerous literary awards.

When asked the obligatory St. Louis question, "Where did you go to high school?" he receives perplexed looks when he responds, "Billings West High." While not a St. Louis native, he has made an extensive study of the city and its fascinating history. Years ago, he developed a website, Tour Saint Louis, and he currently maintains two Facebook pages about St. Louis, St. Louis Sculpture with photos, writeups, and a locator map of over eight hundred sculptures; and St. Louis Secluded Places. He is a Google Maps master reviewer, master photographer and master fact finder, with a half a billion Google Maps photo views of St. Louis. His Facebook page regularly features art, architecture, events and festivals in the St. Louis area, as well as history from across the globe.

https://www.facebook.com/mark.zeman.92